The
Readable Bible

Genesis

GALLEY PROOF
NOT FOR SALE
fcr 03rl

Liddell Press

Also from Liddell Press

The Readable Bible: New Testament

The Readable Bible: Pentateuch

The Readable Bible: Exodus

The Readable Bible: Leviticus

The Readable Bible: Numbers

The Readable Bible: Deuteronomy

The Readable Bible: Psalms

The Anointed One - the complete life of Christ with all the material from the four gospels harmonized in one story.

Visit www.Liddellpress.com for more information.

The Readable Bible

The Readable Bible is primarily a word-for-word translation of the Bible that presents the text in modern formats and renders it as it would be spoken by a native English speaker. Whenever a thought-for-thought translation is presented, the word-for-word translation is footnoted.

Genesis

Rodney S. Laughlin

LIDDELL PRESS
Running for our Lord

Leawood Kansas

Cover/Book Designer/Illustrator: Clyde Adams, www.clydeadams.com

Typeface: Veritas AE from alteredegofonts.com, a division of aespire.com

Printed in the USA   fcr03rl

Contents

Preface..x
   To the Reader..x
   Updates...xi
   Acknowledgments..xi
   Dedication..xi
Introduction to Genesis...xii
Before You Read..xii
The Book of Genesis...1
Genesis Glossary...82
Familiar Verses in Genesis..84
Overlapping Lives of the Patriarchs...87
Measures in Genesis...89
Persons in Genesis...90
Jewish Calendar..94
Subject Index...95
Map Notes...97
Key to Genealogical Tables..97
Translation Notes..98
Format and Presentation Notes...99
Nonliteral Words and Phrases Not Footnoted.....................................100

The Book of Genesis

Maps, tables, and charts are in italics.

Part I: Creation

Genesis 1.. 1
   Creation... 1
Genesis 2.. 2

Part II: The First Humans

   Garden of Eden. Adam and Eve.. 2
Genesis 3.. 3
   The First Sin... 3
   The Curse of Sin 4
Genesis 4.. 5
   Cain and Abel.. 5
   Seth and Enoch Born 5
   Descendants of Adam and Eve... 6

Genesis 5 7
Descendants of Adam 7
Years of the Patriarchs Table 8
Life Spans of the Patriarchs Chart 9
Genesis 6 9
Man's Degradation. Nephilim. 9

Part III: The Life of Noah

Noah Finds Favor 10
Ark Specifications. 10
Genesis 7 10
The Flood. 10
Genesis 8 11
The Flood Recedes. 11
Genesis 9 12
Man Given Dominion 12
Noahic (Rainbow) Covenant. 13
Canaan Cursed 13
Genesis 10 14
Table of the Nations 14
Genesis 11 16
Tower of Babel 16
From Shem to Abram 16

Part IV: The Formation of God's Covenant People

Terah's Journey 17
Genesis 12 17
The Call of Abraham 17
Map: The Life of Abraham 18
Abraham in Egypt. 18
Genesis 13 19
Lot Chooses Sodom. 19
Canaan Promised to Abraham 19
Genesis 14 20
Map: Battle of the Kings 20
Battle of the Kings. Abraham Saves Lot 20
Tithe to Melchizedek 21

Life of Abraham

Genesis 15 22
   God's Covenant with Abraham 22
   Egyptian Bondage and Exodus Foretold 22
   Promised Land Location 22
Genesis 16 23
   Sarai Drives Out Hagar. Ishmael Born 23
Genesis 17 23
   Abram Renamed "Abraham" 23
   Circumcision Covenant 24
   Isaac Promised as Child of the Covenant 24
Genesis 18 25
   Isaac's Birth Foretold 25
   Why God Chose Abraham 25
   Abraham Pleads for the Righteous 25
Genesis 19 26
   Sodom and Gomorrah Destroyed 26
   Moab and Ammon Born Out of Incest 28
Genesis 20 28
   Abraham Calls Sarah His Sister 28
Genesis 21 29
   Birth of Isaac. Hagar and Ishmael Sent Away 29
   Treaty with the Philistines 30
Genesis 22 30
   God Asks Abraham to Sacrifice Isaac 30
   Descendants of Nahor *31*
Genesis 23 32
   Death of Sarah 32
Genesis 24 32
   Servant Sent to Find Isaac a Wife 32
   Isaac Marries Rebekah 35
Genesis 25 36
   Descendants of Abraham *36*
   Abraham Dies. Esau and Jacob Born 37
   Esau Sells His Inheritance 37
Genesis 26 37
   Abrahamic Covenant Reaffirmed to Isaac 37
   Map: The Life of Isaac *38*
   Isaac Calls Rebekah His Sister 38
   God Promises to Bless Isaac 39

Life of Abraham

Life of Isaac

Life of Jacob

Genesis 27..**40**

    Jacob Steals Esau's Blessing...40

    Isaac's Prophecy About Esau...41

    Map: The Life of Jacob..*42*

    Jacob Sent to Laban...43

Genesis 28..**43**

    Jacob's Dream...43

    Abrahamic Covenant Reaffirmed to Jacob....................43

Genesis 29..**44**

    Jacob Marries Leah and Rachel......................................44

    Jacob's Sons..45

Genesis 30..**45**

    Jacob Becomes Rich...46

Genesis 31..**47**

    Jacob Flees Laban..47

    Jacob and Laban Make Peace...48

Genesis 32..**50**

    Jacob Prepares to Meet Esau..50

    Jacob Wrestles and Is Named "Israel"...........................51

Genesis 33..**51**

    Jacob Meets Esau...51

Genesis 34..**52**

    Shechem Rapes Dinah...52

    Simeon and Levi Take Revenge......................................52

Genesis 35..**53**

    Jacob Returns to Bethel...53

    Jacob Reaffirmed as "Israel"..53

    Rachel Dies...54

    Sons of Jacob...*54*

    Isaac Dies..55

Genesis 36..**55**

    Wives and Sons of Esau...*55*

    Jacob and Esau Separate..56

    Sons of Seir..*56*

    Kings of Edom...*57*

    Chiefs of Edom...57

Genesis 37..**57**

    Joseph's Dreams..57

Life of Isaac

Life of Jacob

Life of Joseph

Joseph Sold into Slavery..58
Map: The Life of Joseph..*59*
Genesis 38...60
Judah's Sons...60
Judah and Tamar 60
Genesis 39...61
Joseph and Potiphar's Wife 61
Genesis 40...62
Joseph Interprets the Prisoners' Dreams 62
Genesis 41...63
Joseph Interprets Pharaoh's Dreams 63
Joseph Put Over Egypt 64
Genesis 42...65
Joseph's Brothers Go to Egypt 65
Joseph's Brothers Return to Canaan....................................66
Genesis 43...67
Jacob's Sons Go Back to Egypt...67
Genesis 44...69
Silver Cup in Benjamin's Sack 69
Judah Offers Himself..69
Genesis 45...70
Joseph Reveals Himself..70
Genesis 46...71
Jacob Moves to Egypt 71
Descendants of Jacob..*72*
Genesis 47...74
Joseph's Famine Policies 74
Jacob's Burial Request 75
Genesis 48...76
Jacob Adopts Manasseh and Ephraim. 76
Genesis 49...77
Jacob Blesses His Sons..77
The Death of Jacob 80
Genesis 50...80
Jacob's Burial..80
Joseph's Continuing Forgiveness.......................................81
The Death of Joseph..81

Life of Jacob

Life of Joseph

Preface

To the Reader

One day I was standing in an airport bookstore looking for a book to read. I asked myself, "Why am I looking for something to read when I have a Bible in my briefcase?" I answered, "The Bible is hard to read. I want to read something easier." Then I asked myself, "Why is it so hard to read? You're a seminary graduate, a pastor, a Bible teacher!" Thus began a quest that has led to The Readable Bible, the Bible as it would look if Moses, Joshua, Matthew, Mark, Paul, and the other writers had been sitting in front of a computer when God spoke to them.

It seems to me that the Bible is hard to read because it presents all its material in sentence format. Today we use tables to present census information and charts for genealogies. When we want something built, we draw up a specification document. Law codes are organized in outline form. We use bullet points, bold text, and other aids to help us grasp information. Yet in today's Bibles, all the information is still presented in sentence format in plain text. Surely those men of old would have used modern formats if they had known about them when God spoke to them. Modern formatting does not change the information; it simply presents it in a way that makes it easier to grasp.

Translators have tried to make Scripture easier to read with new translation techniques. The New International Version uses a thought-for-thought method of translating in its effort to achieve functional equivalency. The New Living Translation moves further from the text, so far that many consider it a paraphrase. The Message, marketed as "a contemporary rendering of the Bible," is so far from the original words that a reader often has little idea of what the text actually says. While I lament the movement away from the actual words of the text, I celebrate how much these Bibles have helped people understand the Word of God .

The Readable Bible is just as readable as these new translations, yet it still presents the actual text. This is accomplished by using modern formats and restructuring the text to fit the Western mindset. For instance, topic sentences that are at the end of a paragraph are moved to the front (so sometimes a higher numbered verse appears before a lower numbered one). In those instances when a literal rendering of the text would be misunderstood by most readers, a thought-for-thought translation is rendered and the actual words are footnoted. For instance, the vast majority of readers would not understand that when David wrote, "my kidney instructs me" in Psalm 16, he was referring to his innermost being. Today, if he were a native English speaker, he would say, "my heart instructs me." Thus, "my heart instructs me" is rendered and "my kidney instructs me is footnoted. Read the Translations Principles article and the Formatting and Presentation Notes for more information.

You may struggle with the idea of Scripture in modern formats. Actually, all of today's Bibles present the text in a form much different than that of the original manuscripts. The earliest Hebrew manuscripts have no vowels. They were added hundreds of years later. Neither the Old Testament Hebrew nor the Greek New Testament manuscripts have upper and lower case letters, and they had no punctuation (no commas, no periods!) Chapter numbers were not common in Bibles until the thirteenth century. The first verse numbering system had about one-third of today's verse numbers, making verses three or four times longer. Today's numbering system used in Christian Bibles was not developed until the sixteenth century. The Jewish verse numbering system has 116 more verses in Psalms (because they put verse numbers on the inscriptions at the beginning of each Psalm). Similarly, paragraphing is a later addition to the text, and even today it differs from translation to translation. So dropping text with numbers into tables, cascading the text of long complex sentences, and using other modern formatting techniques is simply continuing the long term trend of making the Bible easier to understand.

We are releasing The Readable Bible in portions as we finish the work. I hope many of you will support this work by preordering your copy of the complete Readable Bible at our website, www.ReadableBible.com.

Our hope is that people who have never read the Bible will decide to read this one because it is so approachable. Please give a copy to someone who does not read the Bible. 09rl

Updates

Register your copy at www.ReadableBible.com. If you opt in, we will offer you the opportunity to purchase our future books of the Bible at a discount when they are released. We will also notify you whenever we post any changes, offer new editions, or post explanatory material on our website or blog. 09rl

Acknowledgments

My thanks to our all the members of our editing team, our volunteer development team, and the many others who have worked to bring The Readable Bible to market.

A bit "thank you" to my designer and partner in this project, Clyde Adams, for joining me in this faith venture. He has turned the translation into well-laid-out text and my formatting concepts into reality. The maps, tables, charts, book layout, and cover are all his work.

Most of all, I thank my wife, Rebecca, for her ideas, her love, and her strong support of this endeavor over the past ten years.

Yet no committee has produced this book. It is ultimately my work, and I accept full responsibility for all its weaknesses. I am sure that the work is not perfect, so I look forward to receiving your constructive criticism at *suggestions@readablebible. com.* 09rl

Dedication

And now I dedicate to our Lord this attempt to translate his Holy Word, humbly asking him to grant that it may bring forth fruit to his glory and the building up of his people. 09rl

April 2018 09rl

Introduction to Genesis[a]

Genesis was written by Moses in the 15th century BC.

Genesis tells us how it all began—the world, man, sin, Israel, and God's first laws for his people. We learn the basics about God, that

He is at the center of all things,
He is in complete control,
He rules over all creation,
He uses flawed persons to bring others to follow him, and
He fulfills his promises.

We discover that people today are no different than people were in the beginning. They lied, cheated, and stole then as we do today. They loved, hated, worked, and connived. They fought wars, tried to outwit each other, and ignored God. But, like today, some chose to follow him and discovered the blessings of believing.

Through it all we find God calling each of us to a life of faith: a life believing that he sees us, cares for us, and is active in our lives.

In chapter 12 God calls Abraham to "leave your country, your people, and your father's house, and go to a country that I will show you." Abraham leaves,with no knowledge of what lies before him other than God's promise to bless him and make him a blessing to others. In the last chapter of Genesis Joseph's brothers come to him in fear, afraid for their lives. They sold him into slavery, and now they expect him to judge them, to exact punishment by making them his slaves. But Joseph says, "Am I in God's place? As for you, you meant evil against me, but God intended it for good. He brought about this present result to save the lives of many. So then, do not be afraid." Genesis is a call for us all to believe like Abraham and Joseph.

Before You Read

Words in *italics* are additions to the biblical text.

Please browse the Glossary before you begin reading. You will find interesting information about words that appear in Genesis frequently, as well as important information regarding the words "Lord" and "Yahweh."

We encourage you to read the Translation Notes article and the Format and Presentation Notes in the back matter. They are easy reading and will increase your understanding of the text.

In the context of commands, rules and regulations, "shall," "must," and "are/is to" are equal terms, all with the same strength of command.

You will also find a helpful Key to Genealogical Tables in the back matter. While we have endeavored to make our tables as intuitive as possible, you may grasp them more quickly if you look at the key first.

---

a "Genesis": a transliterated Greek word that means "origin." The Hebrew Bible title for the book, *bereshit*, (the first word in the Hebrew text) means "in the beginning."

Genesis

Part I: Creation

Genesis 1
Creation

¹ *Day 1:* In the beginning God created the heavens and the earth. ² The earth was formless and empty—darkness was over the surface of the deep—and the Spirit of God hovered over the waters. God said, "Let there be light," and there was light. ⁴ God saw that the light was good, and he separated the light from the darkness. ⁵ God called the light "day" and the darkness "night." And there was evening and morning—the first day.

⁶ *Day 2:* Then God said, "Let there be a space^a between the waters to separate the waters from the vapor.^b Thus, it happened.^c ⁷ God made the space that separated the waters that were under it from the vapor above it. ⁸ God called the space "sky."^d And there was evening and morning—the second day.

⁹ *Day 3:* Then God said, "Let the water under the sky flow^e to one place, and let ground appear." Thus, it happened. ¹⁰ God called the ground "earth," and the gathered waters "seas." And God saw that it was good.

¹¹ Then God said, "Let the land sprout vegetation: seed-bearing plants and trees that bear fruit with seed, each according to its kind on the earth." Thus, it happened. ¹² The land produced vegetation: plants bearing seed according to their kinds and trees bearing fruit with seed according to their kinds. And God saw that it was good. ¹³ And there was evening and morning—the third day.

¹⁴ *Day 4:* Then God said, "Let there be lights in the expanse of the sky to separate the day from the night, and as signs *to mark* seasons, days, and years. ¹⁵ Let them be lights in the expanse of the sky to give light on the earth." Thus, it happened. ¹⁶ God made two great lights—the greater light to govern the day and the lesser light to govern the night—and the stars. ¹⁷ God set them in the expanse of the sky to give light on the earth ¹⁸ to govern the day and the night and to separate light from darkness. And God saw that it was good. ²⁰ And there was evening and morning—the fourth day.

²⁰ *Day 5:* And God said, "Let the water teem with swarms of living creatures, and let birds fly above the earth across the expanse of the sky." ²¹ So God created the great sea creatures and every living creature that moves or swarms in the waters, *all* according to their kind; and every bird after its kind. And God saw that it was good. ²² God blessed them and said, "Be fruitful and increase in number and fill the water in the seas, and let the birds increase upon the earth." ²³ And there was evening and morning—the fifth day.

---

a   Or "expanse." And throughout this "Creation" section.
b   Literally, "waters." And next sentence.
c   Literally, "It was so." And throughout this "Creation" section.
d   Or "heaven."
e   Literally, "be gathered."

1

²⁴ *Day 6:* God said, "Let the land produce living creatures according to their kinds: livestock, reptiles, and wild animals*ᵃ* according to their kinds." Thus, it happened. ²⁵ God made them all*ᵇ* according to their kinds. And God saw that it was good.

²⁶ Then he said, "Let us make humans in our own image, in our own likeness, and let them rule over the fish of the sea, the birds of the air, the livestock, and all the wild animals—over all the earth." ²⁷ So God created mankind in his own image. In the image of God he created them. And he created them male and female.

²⁸ God blessed them and said to them, "Be fruitful and multiply. Fill the earth and subdue it. Rule over the fish of the sea and the birds of the air and over every living creature that moves on the earth." ²⁹ And God said, "Look, I've given you every seed-bearing plant on the face of the whole earth and every tree that has seed-bearing fruit. They'll be food for you. ³⁰ And I am giving all the wild animals and all the birds of the heavens and all the *other* creatures that move on the ground—everything that has the breath of life in it—every green plant for food." Thus, it happened. ³¹ And God saw all that he had made, and it was very good. And there was evening and morning—the sixth day.

Genesis 2

¹ *Day 7:* In this way the heavens and the earth were finished in all their vast array. ² By the seventh day God had completed the work he had been doing, so he rested from all of it.*ᶜ* ³ And God blessed the seventh day and made it holy*ᵈ* because on it he rested from all he had been doing, the work of creation.

Part II: The First Humans

Garden of Eden. Adam and Eve

⁴ This is the account of the creation of the heavens and the earth, *about* when the LORD God made them.*ᵉ* ⁵ No *wild* shrub of the field was on earth, nor had any *grain-producing* plant of the field sprouted, because the LORD God had not sent rain upon the earth. (⁶ Mist*ᶠ* used to come up from the earth and water all the surface of the land.) Now there was no man to work the earth, ⁷ so the LORD God formed man from the dust of the earth and breathed into his nostrils the breath of life, and the man became a living being.

⁸ The LORD God had planted a garden in the east, in Eden, and he put the man he had formed there. ⁹ The LORD God made all kinds of trees grow up from the ground—trees that were pleasing to see and good for food. The tree of life and the tree of knowledge of good and evil were in the middle of the garden. ¹⁰ A river flowing out of Eden watered the garden. Then it divided into four rivers. ¹¹ The first,

---

a   Literally, "beasts of the earth." And throughout this "Creation" section.
b   Literally, "the beasts of the earth according to their kinds, the livestock according to their kinds and everything that creeps on the ground."
c   Literally, "so on the seventh day he rested from all the work which he had done."
d   "Holy": set apart for the purpose(s) and/or service of God.
e   Literally, "when God made the earth and the heavens."
f   Or "wetness," perhaps referring to springs.

named the Pishon, flowed through the entire land of Havilah,*a* where there is gold (¹²the gold of that land is good), aromatic resin, and onyx. ¹³ The second, named the Gihon, flows through the entire land of Cush. ¹⁴ The third, named the Tigris, runs along the east side of Assyria. And the fourth river is the Euphrates.

¹⁵ The LORD God took the man and put him in the Garden of Eden to cultivate it and take care of it. ¹⁶ And the LORD God commanded the man, "Eat freely from any tree in the garden, ¹⁷ but you must not eat from the tree of knowledge of good and evil, for on the day you eat from it you will surely die."

¹⁸ Then the LORD God said, "It is not good for the man to be alone. I will make him a helper*b* to be alongside him."*c*

¹⁹ Now the LORD God had formed out of the ground all the beasts of the field and all the birds of the sky. He brought them to the man to see what he would call them. ²⁰ So the man named them all.*d* But no suitable helper was found for Adam. ²¹ So the LORD God caused the man to fall into a deep sleep. While he slept, God took one of Adam's ribs and then closed up the flesh. ²² Then the LORD God made a woman from the rib taken from the man, and he brought her to the man.

²³ The man said, "This now is bone of my bones and flesh of my flesh. She shall be called 'woman' because she was taken out of man." ²⁴ That is why a man leaves his father and mother and bonds with*e* his wife—and they become one flesh. ²⁵ Though the man and his wife were both naked, they felt no shame.

Genesis 3
The First Sin

¹ Now the serpent was craftier than any of the wild animals the LORD God had made. He asked the woman, "Did God really say 'You must not eat from any tree in the garden?'"

² The woman replied, "We may eat the fruit of the trees in the garden. ³ But God said, 'You must not eat fruit from the tree that is in the middle of the garden, nor touch it, or you will die.'"

⁴ But the serpent said, "You surely will not die! ⁵ For God knows that when you eat from it, your eyes will be opened, and you will be like God—knowing good and evil."

⁶ When she saw that the fruit of the tree was good for food and a delight to the eyes, and also desirable to make one wise, she took *some of* its fruit and ate it. She also gave some to her husband, who was with her, and he ate. ⁷ Then the eyes of both of them were opened, and they realized they were naked; so they sewed fig leaves together to make themselves loincloths.

⁸ Then they heard the sound of the LORD God walking in the garden in the cool of the day. They hid from the LORD God among the trees of the garden, ⁹ but the LORD God called to the man, "Where are you?"

---

a   The Pishon River and Havilah, mentioned here, and the Gihon River and Cush, mentioned in the next sentence, are unknown today. There are several diverse theories about their location.

b   Or "a counterpart." Hebrew: *ezer*, meaning one who acts or intervenes on behalf of or brings benefit to another. It may imply a supplying of what is lacking.

c   Or "to be a counterpart."

d   Literally, "all the livestock, the birds of the sky, and all the wild animals."

e   Or "is united to," or "holds fast to."

¹⁰ He replied, "I heard your voice*ᵃ* in the garden, and I was afraid because I was naked; so I hid."

¹¹ And God said, "Who told you that you were naked? Have you eaten from the tree that I commanded you not to eat from?"

¹² The man said, "The woman you put with me—she gave me *some fruit* from the tree—and I ate it."

¹³ And the LORD God said to the woman, "What have you done?"

And the woman said, "The serpent deceived me, and I ate."

The Curse of Sin

¹⁴ So the LORD God said

> **To the serpent**: "Because you have done this, cursed are you above all the livestock and all the wild animals.*ᵇ* You will crawl on your belly and eat dust all the days of your life. ¹⁵ And I will put enmity*ᶜ* between you and the woman, and between your descendants and her descendants. One of her descendants will crush your head, and you will bruise his heel."
>
> ¹⁶ **To the woman**: "I will greatly increase your pain in childbearing; in pain you will give birth to children. Your desire will be for your husband, and he will rule over you."
>
> ¹⁷ **To Adam**: "Because you listened to your wife and ate from the tree about which I commanded*ᵈ* you (when I said, 'You shall not eat from it'), the ground is cursed because of you. All the days of your life you will eat of its *fruit, but only* through painful toil. ¹⁸ It will sprout thorns and thistles for you. You will eat the plants of the field, ¹⁹ *but only* by the sweat of your brow will you eat your food*ᵉ* until you return to the ground—because from it you were taken, for you are *made from* dust and to dust you will return."

²⁰ Adam*ᶠ* named his wife Eve,*ᵍ* because she would be the mother of all who live.

²¹ The LORD God made garments of skin for Adam and his wife and dressed them. Then the LORD God said, ²² "The man has become like one of us—he *now* knows good and evil. So now he might stretch out his hand and also take and eat *fruit* from the Tree of Life—and he will live forever!" ²³ So the LORD God sent him from the Garden of Eden to work the ground from which he had been taken. ²⁴ He drove the man out and placed cherubim*ʰ* *guards* at the east end of the Garden of Eden and a whirling flaming sword to guard the way to the Tree of Life.

---

a   Or "the sound of you."

b   Literally, "beasts of the field."

c   "Enmity": deep-seated ill will, hatred.

d   Literally, "commanded."

e   Or "bread."

f   "Adam": a transliteration of the Hebrew word for "man."

g   "Eve": a word that has phonetic similarities to the Hebrew verb meaning "to live."

h   "Cherubim": winged angelic beings.

¹ Adam had intimate relations with his wife Eve, and she conceived and gave birth to Cain. And she said, "I have brought forth a man with the help of the LORD." ² *She conceived* again, and she gave birth to his brother, Abel.

Now Abel shepherded*ᵃ* sheep, and Cain cultivated the ground. ³ One day*ᵇ* Cain brought some fruit of the ground as an offering to the LORD, ⁴ and Abel also brought *an offering*—the fat portions of the firstborn of his flock. The LORD approved of*ᶜ* Abel's offering,*ᵈ* ⁵ but he did not approve of Cain and his offering. So Cain was very angry, and he scowled.*ᵉ*

⁶ Then the LORD said to Cain, "Why are you angry? Why the downcast face?*ᶠ* ⁷ If you do what is right, won't you be accepted?*ᵍ* And if you don't do what is right, *remember*, sin is crouching at the door, and it desires to have you, but you must master it."

⁸ *Later* Cain suggested to his brother Abel, "Let's go out to the field."

While they were in the field, Cain attacked Abel and killed him. ⁹ Then the LORD asked Cain, "Where is your brother Abel?"

He replied, "I don't know. Am I my brother's keeper?"

¹⁰ The LORD responded, "What have you done? The voice of your brother's blood cries out to me from the ground. ¹¹ Now you are alienated from the ground which has opened its mouth to receive your brother's blood from your hand. ¹² When you cultivate the ground it will no longer produce good crops*ʰ* for you. You will be a fugitive, a wanderer on the earth."

¹³ Cain replied, "My punishment is too great to bear. ¹⁴ Today you're driving me off the land,*ⁱ* and I will be hidden from your presence.*ʲ* I'll be a vagrant, a wanderer on the earth—and whoever finds me will kill me!"

¹⁵ And the LORD proclaimed, "If anyone kills Cain, sevenfold vengeance will be taken on him." Then the LORD put a mark on Cain so that no one who met him would kill him. ¹⁶ Then Cain went out from the LORD's presence and lived east of Eden in Nod (i.e., Wandering).

Seth and Enoch Born

¹⁷ Cain had intimate relations with his wife, and she conceived and gave birth to Enoch. Then Cain built a city and named it after his son Enoch.

---

a   Or "pastured."
b   Literally, "in the course of time."
c   Literally, "had regard for" or "had feelings toward."
d   Hebrews 11:4 says that Abel offered his sacrifice "by faith."
e   Literally, "his face fell."
f   Literally, "Why has your face fallen?"
g   Literally, "won't you be lifted up?"
h   Literally, "no longer yield its strength."
i   Literally, "from the face of the earth."
j   Literally, "from your face."

Descendants of Adam & Eve 4:1-2, 17-24

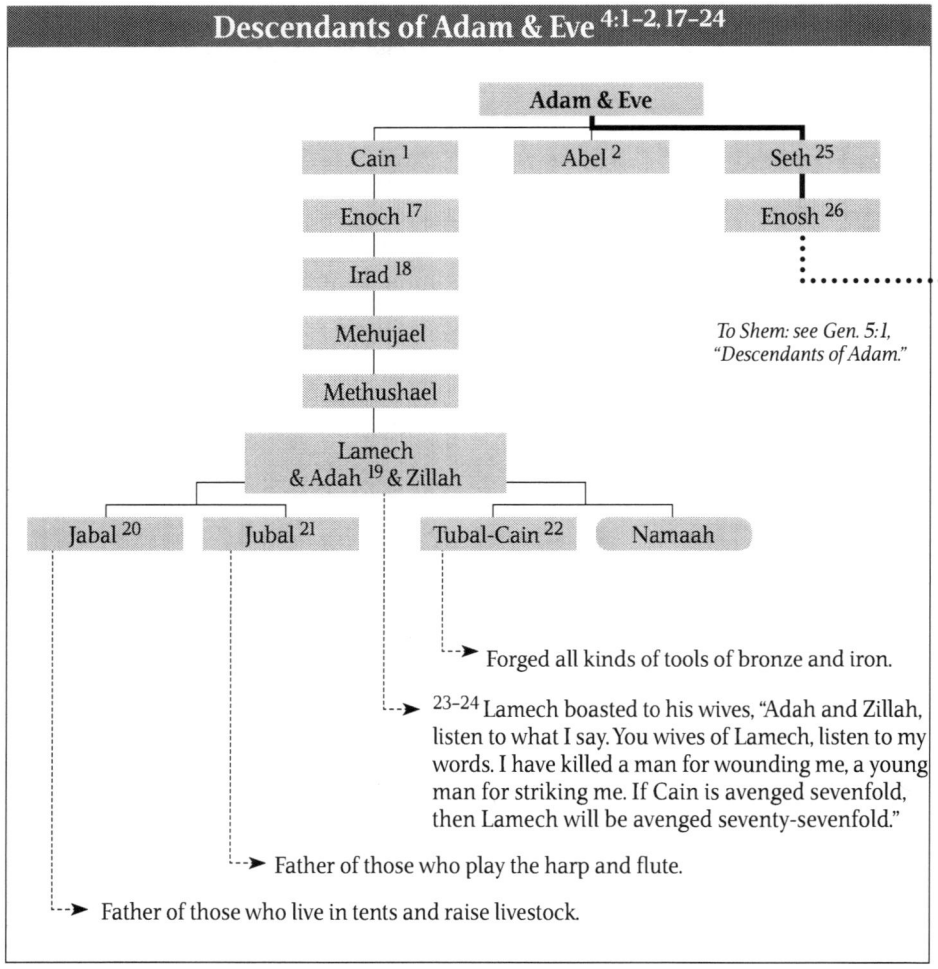

To Shem: see Gen. 5:1, "Descendants of Adam."

Forged all kinds of tools of bronze and iron.

23-24 Lamech boasted to his wives, "Adah and Zillah, listen to what I say. You wives of Lamech, listen to my words. I have killed a man for wounding me, a young man for striking me. If Cain is avenged sevenfold, then Lamech will be avenged seventy-sevenfold."

Father of those who play the harp and flute.

Father of those who live in tents and raise livestock.

25 Adam had intimate relations with his wife again, and she gave birth to a son and named him Seth, *saying,* "God has granted*ᵃ* me another child in place of Abel, since Cain killed him."

26 Seth also had a son, and he named him Enosh. Then men began to call upon the name of the LORD·

---

a   Or "appointed." "Seth" sounds like the Hebrew word for "appointed."

¹ This is the genealogy ª of the descendants of Adam. When God created man, he made him in the likeness of God. ² He created them male and female and blessed them. When they were created, he called them *adam*." ᵇ

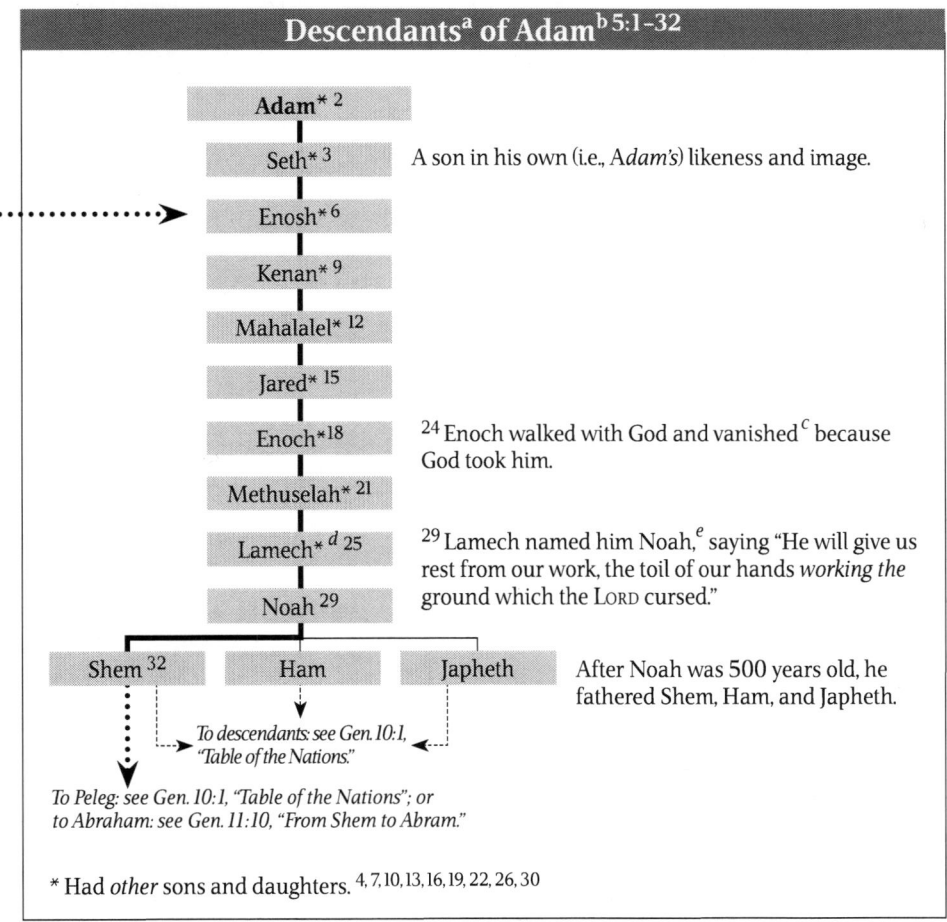

Descendants ª of Adam ᵇ 5:1–32

Adam* 2

Seth* 3 — A son in his own (i.e., Adam's) likeness and image.

Enosh* 6

Kenan* 9

Mahalalel* 12

Jared* 15

Enoch*18 — ²⁴ Enoch walked with God and vanished ᶜ because God took him.

Methuselah* 21

Lamech* ᵈ 25 — ²⁹ Lamech named him Noah, ᵉ saying "He will give us rest from our work, the toil of our hands *working the ground* which the LORD cursed."

Noah 29

Shem 32   Ham   Japheth — After Noah was 500 years old, he fathered Shem, Ham, and Japheth.

To descendants: see Gen. 10:1, "Table of the Nations."

To Peleg: see Gen. 10:1, "Table of the Nations"; or to Abraham: see Gen. 11:10, "From Shem to Abram."

* Had *other* sons and daughters. 4, 7, 10, 13, 16, 19, 22, 26, 30

a   Literally, "the book of the generations."

b   *"Adam"*: a Hebrew word that refers to all the human race.

c   Literally, "and was not."

d   This Lamech is a descendant of Seth. Cain had a descendant named Lamech also.

e   The Hebrew word *Noah* lacks one letter of *nahem*, the Hebrew word meaning "console."

Verse Reference	Patriarch	Birth Year	Age at Birth of Heir	Years Lived After Birth of Heir	Age at Death	Year of Death
Years of the Patriarchs 5:3–32, 11:10–32*						
Years after the creation of Adam						
5:3–5	Adam	0	130	800	930	930
5:6–8	Seth	130	105	807	912	1042
5:9–11	Enosh	235	90	815	905	1140
5:12–14	Kenan	325	70	840	910	1235
5:15–17	Mahalalel	395	65	830	895	1290
5:18–20	Jared	460	162	800	962	1422
5:21–24	Enoch	622	65	300	365	987
5:25–27	Methuselah	687	187	782	969	1656
5:28–31	Lamech	874	182	595	777	1651
5:32; 9:28–29	Noah	1056	502	450	950	2006
11:10–11	Shem	1558	100	500	600	2158
[10] Shem fathered Arphaxad ... two years after the flood.						
11:10–13	Arphaxad	1658	35	403	438	2096
Luke 3:36	Cainan**	1693	33	403	436	2129
11:12–15	Shelah	1726	30	403	433	2159
11:14–17	Eber	1756	34	430	464	2210
11:16–19	Peleg	1790	30	209	239	2029
11:18–21	Reu	1820	32	207	239	2059
11:20–23	Serug	1852	30	200	230	2082
11:22–25	Nahor	1882	29	119	148	2030
11:26, 32	Terah	1911	70	135	205	2116
25:7	Abraham	1981	100	75	175	2156
25:26; 35:28	Isaac	2081	60	120	180	2261
47:28	Jacob	2141	91	56	147	2288
50:26	Joseph	2232	n.a.	n.a.	110	2342

* The verses cited in this heading are rendered only in this table. The verses cited below that are not cited in the heading are also rendered in the normal place.

** Ancient genealogies oftentimes skipped names. Cainan is not mentioned in Genesis but is listed in Matthew's genealogy of Jesus. Cainan's numbers are estimated.

n.a.: not available.
Italicized numbers are calculated, not present in the biblical text.

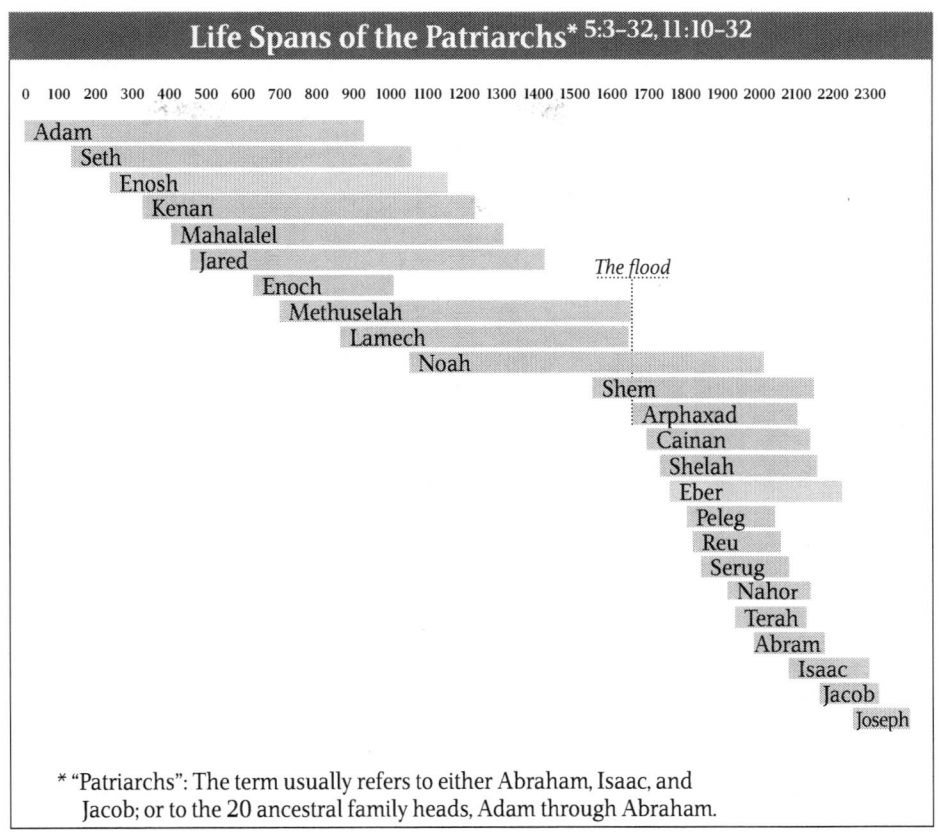

Life Spans of the Patriarchs* 5:3–32, 11:10–32

0   100 200 300 400 500 600 700 800 900 1000 1100 1200 1300 1400 1500 1600 1700 1800 1900 2000 2100 2200 2300

Adam
Seth
Enosh
Kenan
Mahalalel
Jared
Enoch
Methuselah
Lamech
Noah
The flood
Shem
Arphaxad
Cainan
Shelah
Eber
Peleg
Reu
Serug
Nahor
Terah
Abram
Isaac
Jacob
Joseph

* "Patriarchs": The term usually refers to either Abraham, Isaac, and
Jacob; or to the 20 ancestral family heads, Adam through Abraham.

Genesis 6
Man's Degradation. Nephilim

¹ When men began to multiply on the earth and daughters were born to them,
² the sons of God saw that the daughters of men were attractive, and they married
whomever they chose. ³ Then the LORD said, "My Spirit will not strive with mankind
forever, for they are *only mortal* flesh. Their days will be *limited to* a hundred and
twenty years."

⁴ The Nephilim[a] were on the earth in those days, and also afterward. The sons
of God went to the daughters of men and had children by them. They were the heroes
of old, men of renown.

⁵ The LORD saw how great man's wickedness had become on the earth—that
every thought of his heart was always inclined toward evil. ⁶ The LORD was sorry that
he had made man on the earth, and in his heart it grieved him. ⁷ So the LORD said,
"I will wipe out mankind, whom I have made, from the face of the earth—men and
animals (creatures that move along the ground and birds of the air), for I am sorry
that I made them."

---

a   "Nephilim": very large men. See Numbers 13:31–33.

Part III: Life of Noah

Noah Finds Favor

[8] But Noah found favor in the eyes of the LORD. [9] This is the family record of Noah: a righteous man, blameless in his time, who walked with God. [10] Noah had three sons: Shem, Ham, and Japheth.

[11] Now the earth was corrupt in God's sight and it was full of violence. [12] God looked at the earth, and indeed it was corrupt—everyone's behavior was corrupt.[a] [13] God said to Noah, "I have decided to put an end to all creatures;[b] for the earth is filled with violence because of them. I am surely going to destroy *both* them and the earth. [14] So make yourself an ark.[c] Make the ark *this way*:

Ark Specifications 6:14-16	
Material	Gopher* wood [14]
Coating	Pitch, inside and out [14]
Length	450 ft.** [15]
Width	75 ft. [15]
Height	45 ft. [15]
Design	
Rooms in it. [14]	
Roof on it, finished to within one cubit (18 inches) of the top. [16]	
Door in the side. [16]	
Three decks (upper, middle, and lower). [16]	

* "Gopher" is a transliterated Hebrew word. Many believe it refers to cypress wood because that was used for Phoenician ships.
** Literally, "300 cubits." And next two rows, "50 cubits" and "30 cubits."

[17] I—yes, I—am going to bring a flood of water on the earth to wipe out all flesh under the heavens, every living creature[d] that has the breath of life. Everything on earth will perish.

[18] But I will establish my covenant with you. You are to enter the ark—you and your sons and your wife and your sons' wives. [19] You are to bring two of all living creatures, a male and a female, into the ark to keep them alive. [20] Two of every kind of bird and animal and creature that moves along the ground will come to you for you to keep them alive. [21] Take some of every edible food and store it *aboard* for yourself and for them." [22] And Noah did everything, all God had commanded him.

Genesis 7
The Flood

[1] Then the LORD said to Noah, "Go into the ark with your whole family for I have found that of this generation you *alone* are righteous. [2] Take with you every kind of

---

a Literally, "all flesh had corrupted their way."
b Literally, "The end of all flesh has come before me."
c "Ark": The Hebrew word, *aron*, means chest (i.e., box). The first English Bibles transliterated the Latin Vulgate's word, *arcam*, as "ark," and the tradition has continued.
d Literally, "every living thing of all flesh."

- Clean animal:*a* seven pairs, male and female;
- Unclean animal: one pair, male and female; and
- ³ Bird of the sky: seven pairs, male and female,

to keep them alive on the face of the earth. ⁴ For in seven days I will send rain on the earth for forty days and forty nights, and I will wipe off the face of the earth every living thing I have made." ⁵ And Noah did everything that the LORD had commanded him.

⁶ Noah was six hundred years old when the floodwaters came upon the earth. ⁷ And Noah and his wife and his sons and their wives went with him into the ark to escape the floodwaters. ⁸ Pairs of clean and unclean animals, birds and all the creatures that move along the ground, ⁹ male and female, came to Noah and entered the ark, just as God had commanded Noah.

¹⁰⁻¹¹ And after seven days (on the seventeenth day of the second month of the six hundredth year of Noah's life), the springs of the great deep burst open and the floodgates of the heavens were opened, and the floodwaters came upon the earth. ¹³⁻¹⁵ That same day, Noah and his wife and his sons (Shem, Ham, and Japheth) and their three wives and the animals*b* entered the ark—pairs of all flesh in which was the breath of life. ¹⁶ Those that entered were male and female of every living animal.*c* They went in as God had commanded them—and the LORD shut them in. ¹² And the rain fell upon the earth for forty days and forty nights. ¹⁷ For forty days the flood kept coming upon the earth, and the waters increased and lifted up the ark, lifting it above the earth.

¹⁸ The waters prevailed and increased greatly on the earth, and the ark floated on the surface of the water. ¹⁹⁻²⁰ The water overcame *everything,* more and more over the earth until all the high mountains everywhere under the heavens were covered to a depth of more than twenty–two feet.*d* ²¹ All flesh that moved on the earth perished— birds, livestock, wild animals, all the creatures that swarm over the earth, and all mankind. ²² Everything on dry land that had the breath of life in its nostrils died. ²³ God*e* blotted out every living thing that was on the face of the earth: man, animals, creeping things, and birds of the air. Only Noah was left, and those with him in the ark. ²⁴ And the waters prevailed upon the earth for a hundred and fifty days.

Genesis 8
The Flood Recedes

¹⁻² God remembered Noah and all the wild beasts and livestock that were with him in the ark. The fountains of the deep and the floodgates of the heavens were closed, and the rain from the sky was restrained. He sent a wind over the earth, ³ and the waters receded from the earth continually. At the end of a hundred and fifty days it had gone down *considerably.* ⁴ On the seventeenth day of the seventh month the ark came to rest upon the mountains of Ararat. ⁵ The waters continued to go down until the tenth month. On the first day of that month, the tops of the mountains became visible.

---

a   Dietary laws regarding clean and unclean animals are recorded in Leviticus 11 and Deuteronomy 14.

b   Literally, "every beast according to its kind, all the livestock according to their kind, every creeping thing that creeps on the earth according to its kind, and every winged creature."

c   Literally, "all flesh."

d   Literally, "fifteen cubits."

e   Literally, "he."

⁶ After forty days Noah opened the window he had made in the ark ⁷ and he sent out a raven. It flew here and there until the water was dried from the earth. ⁸ Then he sent out a dove to see if the water had receded from the ground's surface. ⁹ Because the water was *still* over all the face of the earth, the dove did not find a resting place for the sole of its feet; so it returned to Noah in the ark. And he put out his hand and brought her back into the ark. ¹⁰ Then he waited seven more days and sent the dove out from the ark again. ¹¹ When the dove returned in the evening, there was a freshly plucked olive leaf in her beak. So Noah knew that the water had receded from the earth. ¹² He waited seven more days and sent the dove out again. And this time it did not return to him.

¹³ In Noah's six hundred and first year, on the first day of the first month, the water had dried up from the earth. Noah removed the ark's covering and saw that the surface of the ground was dry. ¹⁴ On the twenty-seventh day of the second month the earth was dry.

¹⁵ Then God said to Noah, ¹⁶ "Go out of the ark, you and your wife and your sons and their wives. ¹⁷ Bring out every living creature that is with you (birds, animals, creatures that move on the ground) so they swarm upon the earth and are fruitful and multiply." ¹⁸⁻¹⁹ So Noah, his family, and all the animals came out of the ark.*ᵃ*

²⁰ Then Noah built an altar to the LORD, and, using some of the ceremonially clean animals and clean birds, he offered burnt offerings on it. ²¹ When the LORD smelled the pleasing aroma, he said in his heart, "Never again will I curse the ground because of man, even though every intent of his heart is evil from his youth. And I will never again wipe out every living creature as I have done. ²² As long as the earth remains, seedtime and harvest, cold and heat, summer and winter, and day and night will not cease."

Genesis 9
Man Given Dominion

¹ God blessed Noah and his sons and told them, "Be fruitful! Multiply and fill the earth. ² The fear and dread of you will come upon all the beasts of the earth (the birds of the air, everything that creeps on the ground, and all the fish of the sea), for I have given them into your hands. ³ Every moving, living thing will be food for you. Just as I gave you the plants,*ᵇ* I give everything to you. ⁴ But you must not eat meat with its life, its blood, in it.

⁵ "I will surely demand from every animal *that kills a human* a reckoning for your lifeblood. From every person I will demand a reckoning for the life of another person. ⁶ If anyone sheds a person's blood, his blood is to be shed by human *hands* (for God made humans in the image of God). ⁷ As for you, be fruitful and multiply; populate*ᶜ* the earth and increase upon it."

---

a   Literally, "Noah came out, and his sons and his wife and his sons' wives. Every beast, every creeping thing, every bird, everything that moves on the earth, came out by their kinds from the ark."

b   See Genesis 2:16.

c   Literally, "swarm."

⁸ Then God said to Noah and his sons, ⁹ "I hereby establish my covenant with you and with your descendants ¹⁰ and with every living creature that is with you, every beast on earth (birds, livestock, and beasts of the earth—all who came out of the ark with you). ¹¹ I confirm my covenant with you:

- Never again will all living creatures be drowned^a by the waters of a flood;

- Never again will there be a flood to destroy the earth."

¹² And God said, "This is the sign of the covenant that I am making between me and you and every living creature with you for all future generations:

- ¹³ I will place my rainbow in the clouds.

- It will be the sign of my covenant between you and me.

- ¹⁴ Whenever I bring clouds over the earth and the rainbow is seen in the clouds, ¹⁵ I will remember my covenant between me and you and every living creature—all flesh.

- Never again will the waters become a flood to wipe out all flesh.

- ¹⁶ When the rainbow is in the clouds, I will remember the everlasting covenant between God and every kind of living creature—all flesh on earth."

¹⁷ And God said to Noah, "The rainbow is the sign of the covenant I have established with you and all living creatures that are on the earth."

Canaan Cursed

¹⁸⁻¹⁹ The sons of Noah who came out of the ark were Shem, Ham (the father of Canaan), and Japheth. From these three sons of Noah the whole earth was populated.^{b}

²⁰ Noah became a farmer, planted a vineyard, *and made some wine.* ²¹ When he drank some of the wine, he became drunk and lay naked inside his tent. ²² Ham, Canaan's father, saw his father's nakedness and told his two brothers outside. ²³ But Shem and Japheth took a cloak and put it across their shoulder, and then walked in backward and covered their father's nakedness. Their faces were turned away so that they did not see their father's nakedness.

²⁴ When Noah awoke from his drunkenness,^{c} he knew what *Ham,* his youngest son, had done to him. ²⁵ He said, "Cursed be *your oldest son,* Canaan. He will be the lowest of servants^d to his brothers." ²⁶ He also said, "Blessed be the LORD, the God of Shem. Let Canaan be his servant. ²⁷ May God enlarge *the territory of* Japheth. Let him live in the tents of Shem, and let Canaan be his slave."

²⁸ Noah lived 350 years after the flood ²⁹ and died when he was 950 years old.

---

a   Literally, "will all flesh be cut off."
b   Literally, "was scattered."
c   Literally, "wine."
d   Literally, "servant of servants."

Table of the Nations [10:1-32]

[1, 32]The genealogy [a] of Shem, Ham, and Japheth, Noah's sons who had sons born to them after the flood, according to their nations. From these *men* the nations spread over the earth.

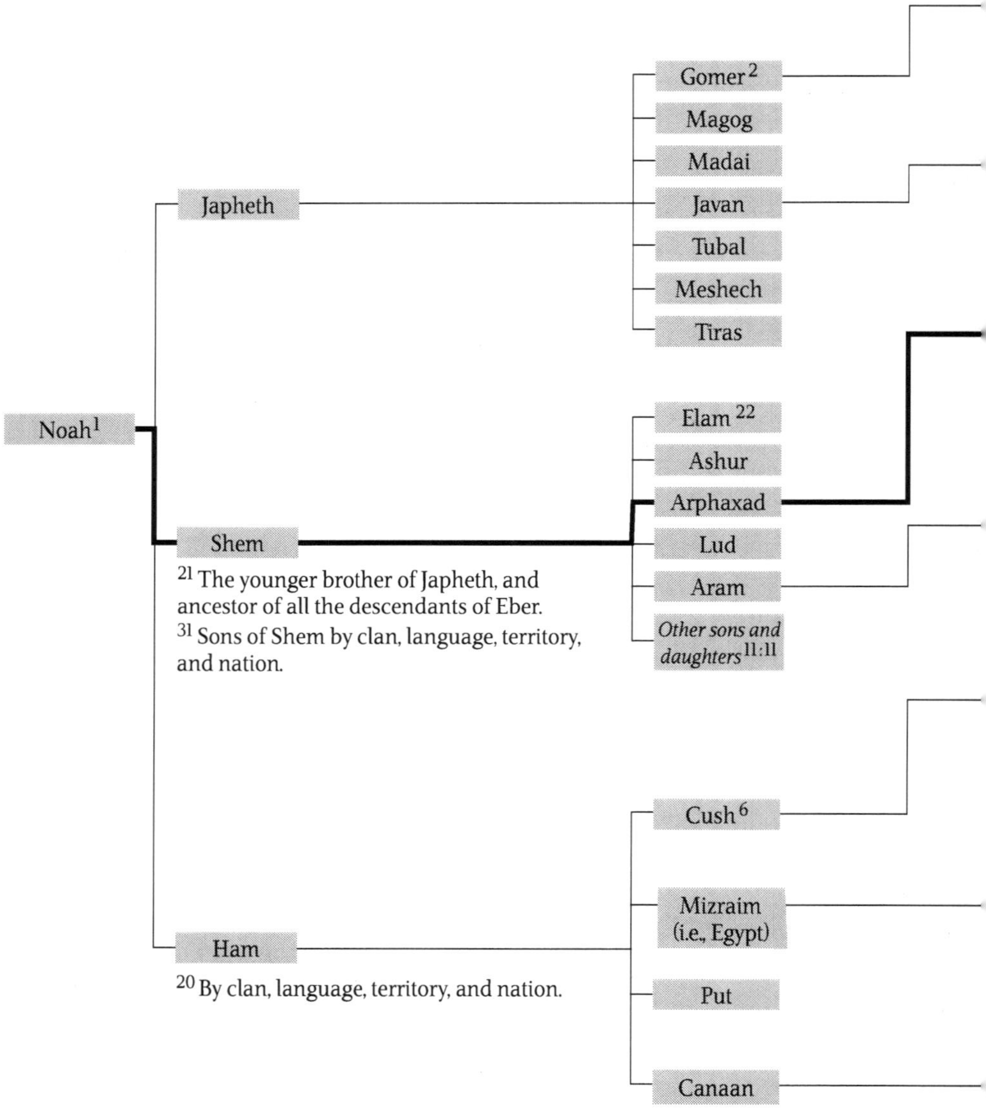

Noah[1]

Japheth
- Gomer[2]
- Magog
- Madai
- Javan
- Tubal
- Meshech
- Tiras

Shem
- Elam [22]
- Ashur
- Arphaxad
- Lud
- Aram
- *Other sons and daughters* [11:11]

[21] The younger brother of Japheth, and ancestor of all the descendants of Eber.
[31] Sons of Shem by clan, language, territory, and nation.

Ham
- Cush[6]
- Mizraim (i.e., Egypt)
- Put
- Canaan

[20] By clan, language, territory, and nation.

[18b] Later the Canaanites spread out. [19] Canaan reached from Sidon toward Gear as far as Gaza, and toward Sodom, Gomorrah, Admah, and Zeboim, as far as Lasha.

[a] Literally, "generations of the sons."

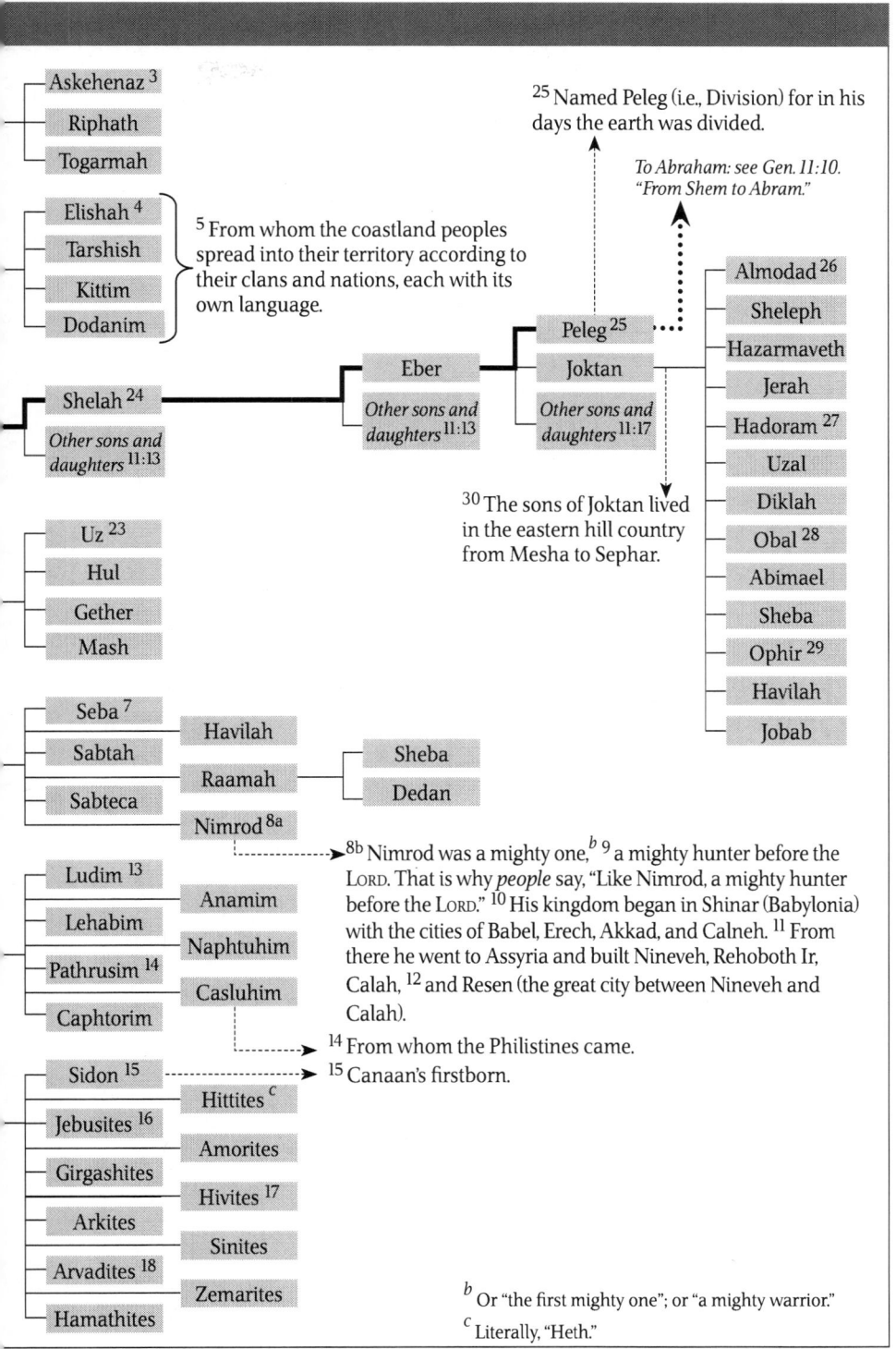

Askehenaz [3]

Riphath

Togarmah

Elishah [4]

Tarshish

Kittim

Dodanim

[5] From whom the coastland peoples spread into their territory according to their clans and nations, each with its own language.

Shelah [24]

Other sons and daughters 11:13

Eber

Other sons and daughters 11:13

Peleg [25]

Joktan

Other sons and daughters 11:17

[25] Named Peleg (i.e., Division) for in his days the earth was divided.

To Abraham: see Gen. 11:10. "From Shem to Abram."

Almodad [26]

Sheleph

Hazarmaveth

Jerah

Hadoram [27]

Uzal

Diklah

Obal [28]

Abimael

Sheba

Ophir [29]

Havilah

Jobab

[30] The sons of Joktan lived in the eastern hill country from Mesha to Sephar.

Uz [23]

Hul

Gether

Mash

Seba [7]

Sabtah

Sabteca

Havilah

Raamah

Nimrod [8a]

Sheba

Dedan

[8b] Nimrod was a mighty one,[b] [9] a mighty hunter before the Lord. That is why *people* say, "Like Nimrod, a mighty hunter before the Lord." [10] His kingdom began in Shinar (Babylonia) with the cities of Babel, Erech, Akkad, and Calneh. [11] From there he went to Assyria and built Nineveh, Rehoboth Ir, Calah, [12] and Resen (the great city between Nineveh and Calah).

Ludim [13]

Lehabim

Pathrusim [14]

Caphtorim

Anamim

Naphtuhim

Casluhim

[14] From whom the Philistines came.

Sidon [15]

Jebusites [16]

Girgashites

Arkites

Arvadites [18]

Hamathites

Hittites [c]

Amorites

Hivites [17]

Sinites

Zemarites

[15] Canaan's firstborn.

[b] Or "the first mighty one"; or "a mighty warrior."

[c] Literally, "Heth."

Genesis 11
Tower of Babel

¹ Now the whole world had one language and the same words. ² When people journeyed east and found the plain of Shinar and settled there, ³ they said to each other, "Here, let's make bricks and bake them hard."*a* They used brick instead of stone, and tar for mortar. ⁴ Then they said, "Here, rather than be scattered over the whole earth, let's build a city for ourselves with a tower with its top in the heavens to make a name for ourselves."

---

a   Literally, "bake them thoroughly."

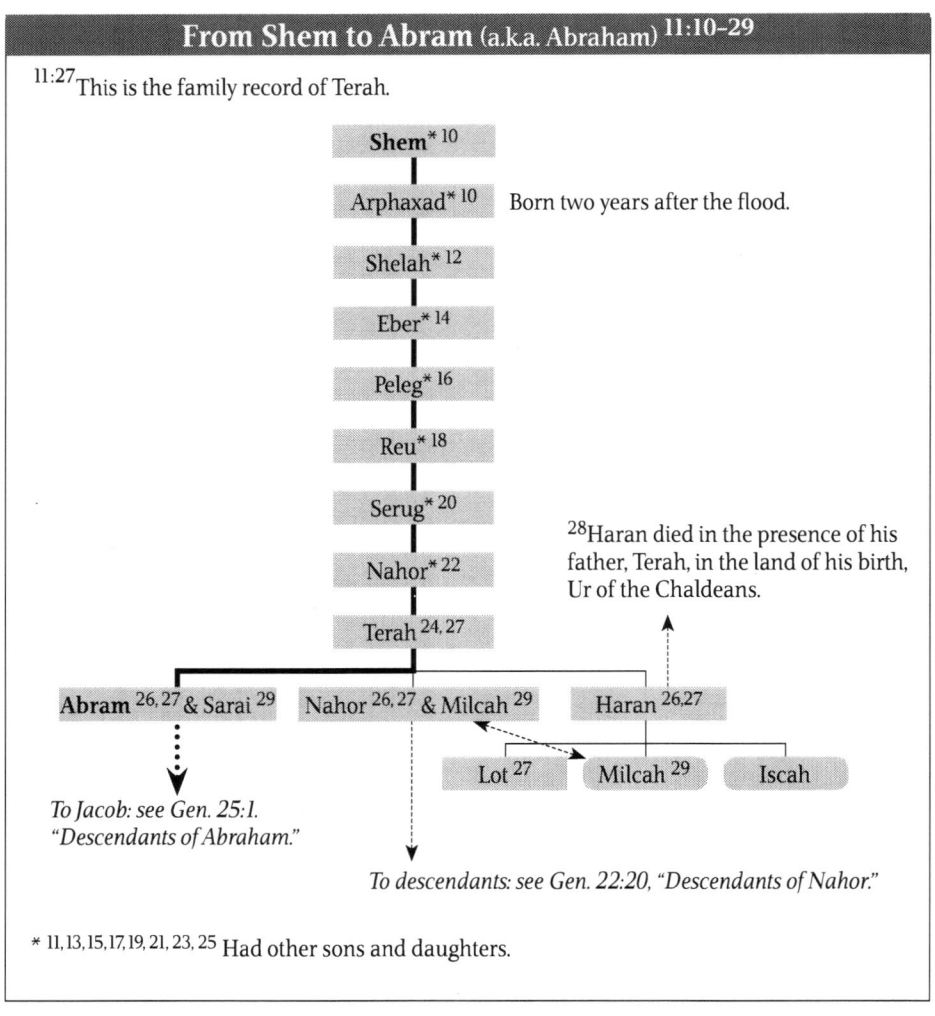

From Shem to Abram (a.k.a. Abraham) **11:10–29**

11:27 This is the family record of Terah.

Shem* 10

Arphaxad* 10   Born two years after the flood.

Shelah* 12

Eber* 14

Peleg* 16

Reu* 18

Serug* 20

Nahor* 22   ²⁸Haran died in the presence of his father, Terah, in the land of his birth, Ur of the Chaldeans.

Terah 24, 27

Abram 26, 27 & Sarai 29   Nahor 26, 27 & Milcah 29   Haran 26,27

Lot 27   Milcah 29   Iscah

To Jacob: see Gen. 25:1. "Descendants of Abraham."

To descendants: see Gen. 22:20, "Descendants of Nahor."

* 11, 13, 15, 17, 19, 21, 23, 25 Had other sons and daughters.

⁵ But the LORD came down to see the city and the tower that the children of man were building. ⁶ He said, "Look, they are one people and have one language—and this is what they do! Now nothing which they propose to do will be impossible for them. ⁷ Come, let's go down there and confuse their language so they will not understand each other."

So the LORD scattered them from there over the whole earth, and they stopped building the city. ⁹ That is why it was called Babel,ᵃ because there the LORD confused the language of the whole earth. And from there the LORD scattered them over the face of all the earth.

Verses 10–29 are in "From Shem to Abram" above.

Part IV: The Formation of God's Covenant People

Terah's Journey

³⁰ Now Sarai was unable to conceive, and she had no child. ³¹ Terah set out from Ur of the Chaldeans with his son Abram and his daughter-in-law Sarai and his grandson Lot to go to the land of Canaan. But when they came to Haran, they settled there. ³² Terah lived for 205 years, and he died in Haran.

Genesis 12
The Call of Abrahamᵇ

¹ The LORD said to Abram, "Leave your country, your people, and your father's house, and go to the land that I will show you. ² I will make you into a great nation, and I will bless you and make your name great. You will be a blessing, ³ and I will bless those who bless you and curse those who curse you. And through you all the peoples on earth will be blessed."

⁴ So Abram, seventy-five years old, left as the LORD had told him. ⁵ He took his wife Sarai, his nephew Lot, all the possessions they had accumulated, and the people they had acquiredᶜ in Haran, and set out for the land of Canaan. When they arrived there,ᵈ ⁶ *even though* the Canaanites were in the land, Abram went as far as Shechem (by the oakᵉ of Moreh). ⁷ There the LORD appeared to him and said, "I will give this land to your descendants." So there he built an altar to the LORD, who had appeared to him.

⁸ Then he went toward the hill countryᶠ east of Bethel and west of Ai and pitched his tent. There he built an altar to the LORD and called upon the name of the LORD. ⁹ Then Abram set out and continued *south* toward the Negev.

---

a   Or "Babylon"; or "Babylonia."
b   Abraham, named "Abram" (*i.e.*, exalted father) at birth, was renamed "Abraham" (*i.e.*, father of many) in Genesis 17.
c   Or "people they had made." The Talmud says these were people they had led to follow the Lord.
d   Literally, "in the land of Canaan."
e   Or "terebinth," a smaller tree. Oak and terebinth trees often grow in the same area.
f   Or "the mountain."

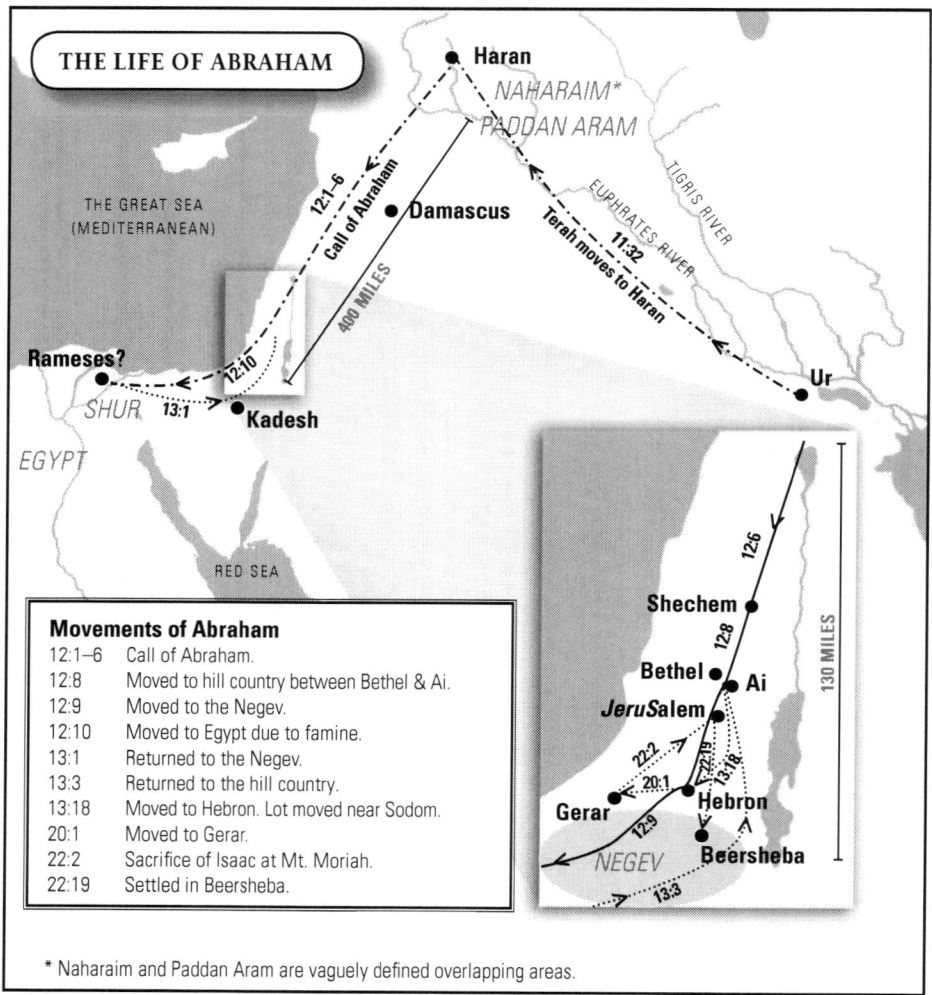

THE LIFE OF ABRAHAM

THE GREAT SEA
(MEDITERRANEAN)

Haran

NAHARAIM*

PADDAN ARAM

TIGRIS RIVER

EUPHRATES RIVER

12:1-6
Call of Abraham

Damascus

Terah moves to Haran
11:32

400 MILES

Ur

Rameses?

12:10

SHUR   13:1   Kadesh

EGYPT

RED SEA

Movements of Abraham

12:1–6	Call of Abraham.
12:8	Moved to hill country between Bethel & Ai.
12:9	Moved to the Negev.
12:10	Moved to Egypt due to famine.
13:1	Returned to the Negev.
13:3	Returned to the hill country.
13:18	Moved to Hebron. Lot moved near Sodom.
20:1	Moved to Gerar.
22:2	Sacrifice of Isaac at Mt. Moriah.
22:19	Settled in Beersheba.

12:6

Shechem

12:8

130 MILES

Bethel   Ai

JeruSalem

22:2

20:1

13:18

Gerar   12:9   Hebron

NEGEV   Beersheba

13:3

* Naharaim and Paddan Aram are vaguely defined overlapping areas.

Abraham in Egypt

¹⁰ Now there was a famine in the land. Because the famine was severe, Abram went down to Egypt to live there temporarily. ¹¹ When they were about to enter Egypt, he said to his wife Sarai, "Look, I know what a beautiful woman you are. ¹² When the Egyptians see you, they will say, 'This is his wife,' and they will kill me but let you live. ¹³ Please say that you are my sister so my life will be spared for your sake."[a]

¹⁴ When Abram entered Egypt, the Egyptians did notice that Sarai was a very beautiful woman. ¹⁵ Pharaoh's officials saw her and expressed admiration of her to Pharaoh, and she was taken into his palace. ¹⁶ For her sake he treated Abram well by giving him sheep and cattle, male and female donkeys, male and female servants,[b]

---

a Literally, "Please say that you are my sister so my life will be spared for your sake, and so my life will be spared on account of you."

b Or "slaves."

and camels. [17] But the LORD struck Pharaoh and his house with great plagues because of Abram's wife Sarai. [18] So Pharaoh summoned Abram and said, "What have you done to me? [19] Why didn't you tell me she was your wife? Why did you say, 'She is my sister,' so that I took her as a wife? Now then, here is your wife. Take her and get out." [20] Then Pharaoh gave orders about him to his men, and they sent him on his way with his wife and all he had.

Genesis 13
Lot Chooses Sodom

[1-2] Abram, who had become very rich in livestock and silver and gold, went up from Egypt to the Negev with his wife and Lot and all he had. [3] From the Negev he went past Bethel to the place between Bethel and Ai (where his tent had been at the beginning, [4] where he had first built an altar). There Abram called upon the name of the LORD.

[5] Now Lot, who went with Abram, also had flocks and herds and tents. [6] Their possessions were so great that the land could not support them living there together. [7] Also, there was strife between Abram's and Lot's herdsmen, and the Canaanites and Perizzites were living there.[a] [8] So Abram said to Lot, "Please, let's not have any strife between you and me, or between my herdsmen and yours, for we are brothers. [9] Isn't the whole land available to you?[b] Let's separate. If you go to the left, I'll go to the right. If you go to the right, I'll go to the left."

[10] Lot lifted his eyes and saw that all the plain of the Jordan was well watered everywhere, like the garden of the LORD, like the land of Egypt toward Zoar. (This was before the LORD destroyed Sodom and Gomorrah.) [11] So Lot chose for himself the whole Jordan plain and went east, and they separated from each other. [12] Abram lived in the countryside of Canaan, while Lot lived in the cities of the plain and pitched his tents next to Sodom. [13] Now the men of Sodom were wicked and were sinning exceedingly against the LORD.

Canaan Promised to Abraham

[14] The LORD said to Abram after Lot had departed, "Lift up your eyes and look[c] to the north and south and to the east and west. [15] I am giving you and your descendants forever all the land that you see. [16] I will make your descendants like the dust of the earth, so that if anyone could count the earth's dust particles,[d] then your descendants could also be counted. [17] Get up and walk throughout the length and breadth of the land, for I am giving it to you."

[17] So Abram moved his tent and went to live by the oaks of Mamre at Hebron. And there he built an altar to the LORD.

---

a   Literally, "in the land."
b   Literally, "the whole land before you."
c   Literally, "look from the place where you are."
d   Literally, "the dust of the earth."

Genesis 14
Battle of the Kings. Abraham Saves Lot

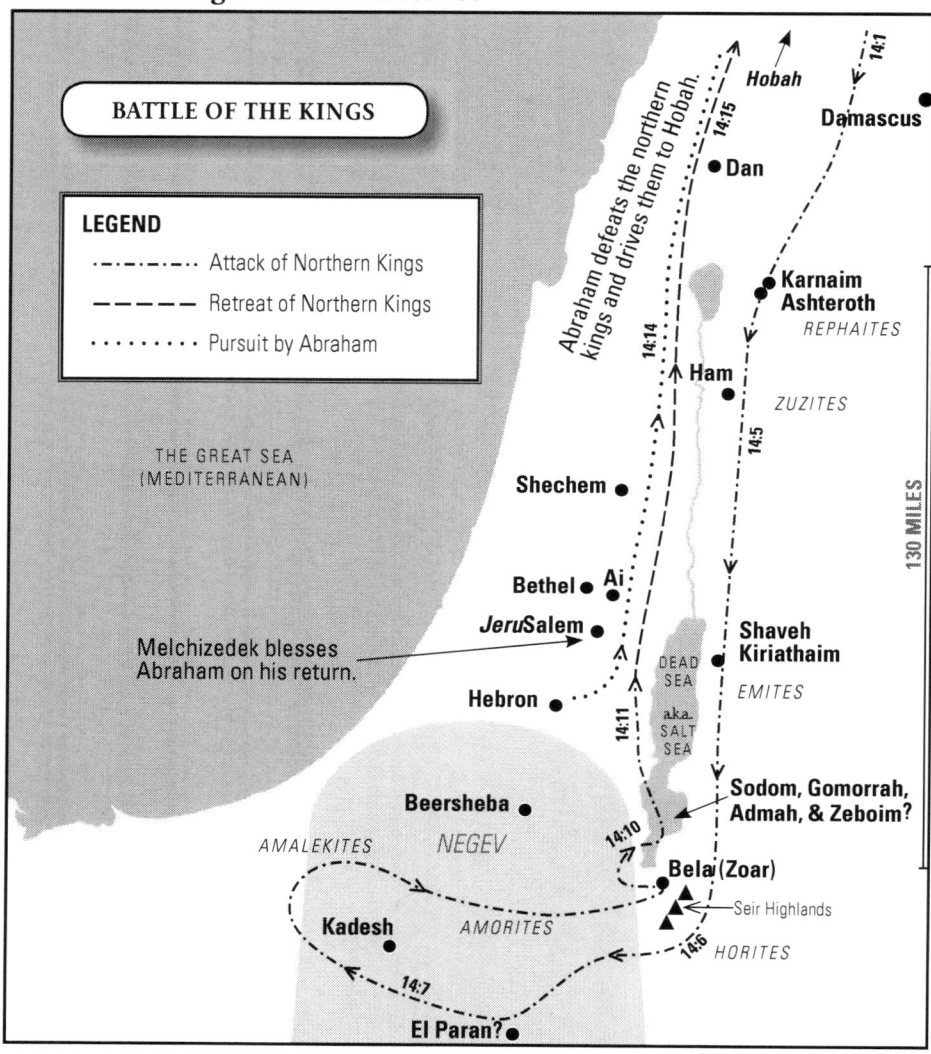

BATTLE OF THE KINGS

LEGEND
- —·—·—·—· Attack of Northern Kings
- — — — — — Retreat of Northern Kings
- · · · · · · · · · Pursuit by Abraham

THE GREAT SEA
(MEDITERRANEAN)

Abraham defeats the northern
kings and drives them to Hobah.

14:1

Hobah

Damascus

Dan

14:15

14:14

Karnaim
Ashteroth

REPHAITES

Ham

ZUZITES

14:5

Shechem

130 MILES

Bethel • Ai

*Jeru*Salem

Melchizedek blesses
Abraham on his return.

Shaveh
Kiriathaim

DEAD
SEA

EMITES

Hebron

14:11

a.k.a.
SALT
SEA

Beersheba

Sodom, Gomorrah,
Admah, & Zeboim?

AMALEKITES *NEGEV*

14:10

Bela (Zoar)

Seir Highlands

Kadesh   *AMORITES*

14:6 *HORITES*

14:7

El Paran?

The Battling Kings

Each place the term "northern kings" or "kings of the Dead Sea Valley" appears in this chapter, in the biblical text the kings are all listed as below:

Northern Kings	**Kings of the Dead Sea Valley**
Amraphel, king of Shinar (a.k.a. *Babylonia*)	Bera, king of Sodom
	Birsha, king of Gomorrah
Arioch, king of Ellasar	Shinab, king of Admah
Chedorlaomer, king of Elam*	Shemeber, king of Zeboiim
Tidal, king of Goiim	*Name unknown,* king of Bela (i.e., Zoar)
* A kingdom just north of Babylonia	

¹ It came about in those days that *the northern kings* ² went to war with the *kings of the Dead Sea Valley.* ⁴⁻⁵ In their thirteenth year of serving Chedorlaomer,ᵃ ⁵ the *kings of the Dead Sea Valley*ᵇ joined together in the Valley of Siddim (*i.e.,* the Salt Sea) and rebelled.

⁵ In the fourteenth year the *northern kings* defeated the Rephaites in *the twin cities of* Ashteroth *and* Karnaim, the Zuzites in Ham, the Emites in Shaveh Kiriathaim, ⁶ and the Horites in the Seir Highlands—*conquering* as far as El Paran (in the wilderness). ⁷ Then they turned back to En Mishpat (*i.e.,* Place of Judgement; a.k.a. Kadesh, *i.e.,* Holy) and conquered the Amalekites and the Amorites who were living in Hazazon Tamar.

⁸⁻⁹ Then *the army of the* five *kings of the Dead Sea Valley* marched out and drew up their battle lines against the *army of the* four *northern kings* in the Valley of Siddim. ¹⁰ The *armies of the* kings of Sodom and Gomorrah fled to the hill country, and some fell into the many tar pits of the Valley of Siddim. ¹¹ The *northern kings* seized all the goods and food of Sodom and Gomorrah and left. ¹² When they departed, they also took Abram's nephew Lot and his possessions, for he was living in Sodom.

¹³ An escapee came and reported this to Abram the Hebrew when he was living *around Hebron* near the oaks of Mamre.ᶜ ¹⁴ When Abram heard that his relative had been captured, he called out the 318 trained men born in his house and pursued *the northern kings north* as far as Dan. ¹⁵ *There* he divided his men, attacked during the night, and defeated *the northern forces* and pursued them north of Damascus as far as Hobah. ¹⁶ Then he recovered all the goods and brought back his nephew Lot, his women and people, and his possessions.

¹⁷ After returning from the defeat of Chedorlaomer and the kings allied with him, the king of Sodom went out to meet Abram in the Valley of Shaveh (*i.e.,* Valley of the Kings).ᵈ

Tithe to Melchizedek

¹⁸ Melchizedek, king of Salem,ᵉ a priest of God Most High, brought out bread and wine ¹⁹ and blessed Abram, saying: "Praise be to Abram by God Most High, Creatorᶠ of heaven and earth. ²⁰ And blessed beᵍ God Most High, who delivered your enemies into your hand." Then Abram gave him a tenth of everything.

²¹ The king of Sodom said, "Give the people to me and keep the goods for yourself."

²² But Abram replied to him, "I have swornʰ to the Lᴏʀᴅ, God Most High, Creator of heaven and earth, ²³ that I will accept nothing of yours, not even a thread or the strap of a sandal, so that you will never be able to say, 'I made Abram rich.' ²⁴ I will accept nothing except what the young men have eaten and the share that belongs to the men who went with me—Aner, Eshcol, and Mamre. Let them take their share."

---

a   Literally, "They had served Chedorlaomer for twelve years, but in the thirteenth year."
b   Literally, "these."
c   Literally, "the oaks of Mamre (*who was an* Amorite relative of Eshcol and Aner, allies of Abram)."
d   "Valley of the Kings": Located next to Salem (a.k.a. Jerusalem).
e   Or "king of peace." "Peace" is used in the sense of prosperity and well-being.
f   Or "possessor."
g   Or "praise be to."
h   Literally, "lifted my hand."

Genesis 15
God's Covenant with Abraham

¹ After this, the word of the LORD came to Abram in a vision: "Do not be afraid, Abram. I am your shield, your reward will be very great.*ᵃ*

² But Abram said, "O LORD God,*ᵇ* what can you give me since I am childless? The heir of my estate*ᶜ* is *my chief servant,* Eliezer of Damascus. ³ Since you haven't given me any children, a servant in my household will be my heir."

⁴ Then the word of the LORD came to him: "This man will not be your heir, but a son coming from your own body will be your heir." ⁵ God took him outside and said, "Look toward the heavens*ᵈ* and count the stars—if you are able to count them. That's how many descendants you will have."*ᵉ* ⁶ Abram believed the LORD, and God counted him as righteous because of his faith.*ᶠ*

⁷ Then God said, "I am the LORD, who brought you out of *the city of* Ur of the Chaldeans (*i.e., Babylonia*) to give you this land to possess it."

⁸ But Abram replied, "O LORD God, how can I know that I will possess it?"

⁹ The LORD responded, "Bring me a young cow, a goat, and a ram, each three years old, along with a dove and a young pigeon."

¹⁰ Abram brought all these to him, cut them in two, and laid each half opposite the other. The birds, however, he did not cut in half. ¹¹ Then vultures came down on the carcasses, but Abram drove them away.

Egyptian Bondage and Exodus Foretold

¹² When the sun was setting, Abram fell into a deep sleep, and a terrible dreadful darkness came over him. ¹³ Then the LORD said, "Know for certain that your descendants will be strangers in a country that is not theirs, and they will be enslaved and oppressed for four hundred years. ¹⁴ But I will punish the nation they serve, and afterward they will come out with great possessions. ¹⁵ You, however, will die*ᵍ* in peace and be buried at a good old age. ¹⁶ In the fourth generation your descendants will return here, for the sin of the Amorites is not complete." ¹⁷ When the sun had set and darkness had fallen, a smoking oven and a blazing torch *appeared* and passed between the pieces.*ʰ*

Promised Land Location

¹⁸ On that day the LORD made a covenant with Abram, saying, "I have given this land to your descendants: from *the Nile,* the river of Egypt, as far as the great river, *the Euphrates* (¹⁹ *the land occupied by* the Kenites, Kenizzites, Kadmonites, Hittites, Perizzites, Rephaites, ²⁰ Amorites, Canaanites, Girgashites, and Jebusites)."

---

a   Or "your very great reward."
b   Or "Sovereign LORD."
c   Literally, "house."
d   Or "toward heaven."
e   Literally, "so shall your descendants be."
f   Literally, "God credited it to him as righteousness."
g   Literally, "go to your fathers."
h   See "Covenant" in the Glossary for an explanation.

Sarai Drives Out Hagar. Ishmael Born

¹ Now Abram had been living in Canaan for ten years, and his wife Sarai had not *been able* to bear him any children. But she had an Egyptian maidservant named Hagar. ² So she said to Abram, "Since the LORD has kept me from having children, go sleep with my maidservant. Perhaps I can build *a family* through her." And Abram listened to the voice of Sarai. ³ And she gave him Hagar as his wife.ᵃ ⁴ And he slept with her, and she conceived.

When Hagar knew she was pregnant, she began to despiseᵇ her mistress. ⁵ So Sarai complained to Abram, "You are responsible for the wrong I am suffering.ᶜ I put my servant in your arms. Then she saw that she is pregnant. And now she looks down on me!ᵈ May the LORD judge between you and me."

⁶ Abram responded, "Your servant is in your hands. Do with her whatever you want."ᵉ So Sarai mistreated Hagar and she fled.ᶠ

⁷ The angel of the LORD found Hagar near a desert spring on the way to Shur, ⁸ and he asked, "Hagar, servant of Sarai, where have you come from, and where are you going?"

She replied, "I am running away from my mistress, Sarai."

⁹ The angel of the LORD instructed her, "Go back to your mistress and submit to her authority. ¹⁰ I will multiply your descendants so that there will be too many to count. ¹¹ Now you are pregnant, and you will have a son. Name him Ishmael (*i.e.*, God Hears), because the LORD has heard your *cry of* distress.ᵍ ¹² He will be a wild donkey of a man. His hand will be against everyone, and their hands will be against him, and he will live in ill-disposed towardstʰ all his brothers."

¹³ Hagar named the LORD who spoke to her El Roi (*i.e.*, The God Who Sees Me), for she said, "I have seen him who sees me." ¹⁴ That is why the well was called Beer Lahai Roi (*i.e.*, Well of the Living One Who Sees Me). The well is still there, between Kadesh and Bered. ¹⁵⁻¹⁶ And Hagar bore Abram a son when he was eighty-six years old, and Abram named him Ishmael.

Genesis 17
Abram Renamed "Abraham"

¹ When Abram was ninety-nine years old, the LORD appeared to him and said, "I am El Shaddai (*i.e.*, God Almighty). Walk before me and be blameless. ² I will establish my covenantⁱ between me and you and will multiply you exceedingly."

---

a Literally, "And she gave her Egyptian maidservant Hagar to her husband Abram as his wife." Common law in ancient Mesopotamia allowed a barren woman to give her slave to her husband and recognize their child as her own.

b "Despise": express an attitude of hatred or disgust toward something because it is seen as worthless or undeserving of respect.

c Literally, "may the wrong done to me be upon you."

d Literally, "I am despised in her eyes."

e Literally, "whatever is good in your sight."

f Literally, "fled from her face."

g Literally, "heard your affliction."

h Literally, "live opposite from," which might mean "to the east of."

i Or "be blameless that I may establish my covenant."

³ "Abram fell on his face, and God continued, ⁴ "As for me, this is my covenant with you: You will be the father of many nations. ⁵ You will no longer be called Abram (i.e., Exalted Father), but your name will be Abraham (i.e., Father of Many) for I have made you a father of many nations. ⁶ I will make you exceedingly fruitful. I will make nations of you, and kings will come forth from you. ⁷ I will establish my covenant as an everlasting covenant between me and you and your descendants, to be your God and the God of your descendants*a* after you. ⁸ I will give you and your descendants forever the whole land of Canaan, where you are now living as foreigners, as an everlasting possession. And I will be their God.

Circumcision Covenant

⁹ "As for you, you must keep my covenant, you and your descendants forever. ¹⁰ This is my covenant with you and your descendants, the covenant you are to keep: Every male among you is to be circumcised. ¹¹ You must be circumcised in the flesh of your foreskin, and it will be the sign of the covenant between me and you.

¹² For the generations to come, every male among you who is eight days old must be circumcised, *including servants* born in your house or bought with money from a foreigner who is not your descendant. ¹³ Those born in your house and bought with your money are to be circumcised. My covenant in your flesh is to be an everlasting covenant. ¹⁴ Any uncircumcised male who is not circumcised in the flesh of his foreskin is to be cut off from his people *because* he has broken my covenant.

Isaac Promised as Child of the Covenant

¹⁵ "As for your wife Sarai, you are no longer to call her Sarai. Her name will be Sarah (i.e., Princess).*b* ¹⁶ I will bless her and will surely give you a son by her. I will bless her, and she will be *the mother* of nations. Kings of peoples will come from her."

¹⁷ Abraham fell on his face, laughed, and said in his heart, "Will a son be born to a hundred-year-old man? Will Sarah bear a child when she is ninety years old?" ¹⁸ And he said to God, "Oh, that Ishmael might live under your blessing!"*c*

¹⁹ But God said, "No, but your wife Sarah will bear you a son, and you will call him Isaac (i.e., He Laughs). I will establish my covenant with him as an everlasting covenant for his descendants. ²⁰ As for Ishmael, I have heard you. Look, I will bless him—make him fruitful and multiply his descendants.*d* He will father twelve princes, and I will make him into a great nation. ²¹ But I will establish my covenant with Isaac, whom Sarah will bear to you at this time next year." ²² When he had finished speaking, God went up from Abraham.

²³⁻²⁷ On that very day Abraham (who was ninety-nine years old) took his son Ishmael (who was thirteen years old) and all those born in his household or bought with money (*including those* bought from a foreigner), every male in his household, and circumcised the flesh of the foreskin of himself and them as God had told him.*e*

---

a   Literally, "to be God to you and your descendants."
b   Or "mistress," in the sense of ruling, as in "mistress of the house."
c   Literally, "live before you."
d   Literally, "his numbers."
e   These four verses contain many duplicated phrases. Each phrase is rendered only one time.

Isaac's Birth Foretold

¹ The Lord appeared to Abraham in the heat of the day while he was sitting at the entrance to his tent near the great trees of Mamre. ² When Abraham looked up, three men (*the Lord and two angels*[a]) were standing before him. When he saw them, he ran from the tent door to meet them and bowed low and said, ³ "My lord, if I have found favor in your sight, please do not pass by your servant. ⁴ Let a little water be brought and wash your feet and rest yourselves under this tree. ⁵ I will bring you a bit of food, and you can refresh yourselves. After that you may go on your way, since you *have honored* your servant with this visit."

So they said, "Do as you have said."

⁶ So Abraham hurried into the tent and said to Sarah, "Quick, get three measures[b] of fine flour, knead it, and bake some bread."

⁷ Then he ran to the herd and selected a choice, tender calf and gave it to a servant, who hurried to prepare it. ⁸ When it was prepared, he brought out the calf, along with some curds and milk. After setting these before them, he stood under a nearby tree while they ate.

⁹ They asked him, "Where is your wife Sarah?"

He replied, "There, in the tent."

¹⁰ The Lord said, "I will surely return to you about this time next year, and Sarah, your wife, will have a son." Sarah was behind him, listening at the tent entrance.

¹¹ Now Abraham and Sarah were old and advanced in years, and Sarah was past childbearing.[c] ¹² And she laughed to herself, thinking, "After I am shriveled and my lord is old, I will have such pleasure?"

¹³ Then the Lord[d] said *to Abraham*, "Why did Sarah laugh, saying, 'Will I really have a child when I am so old?' ¹⁴ Is anything too hard for the Lord? I will return to you at this time next year, and Sarah will have a son."

¹⁵ Sarah was afraid, so she lied, saying, "I didn't laugh."

But he said, "No, you did laugh."

Why God Chose Abraham

¹⁶ When the *Lord and the two* men got up to leave and looked down toward Sodom, Abraham walked up to say goodbye.[e] ¹⁷ The Lord thought, "Shall I hide from him what I am about to do? ¹⁸ For he will surely become a great and powerful nation, and all nations will be blessed through him. ¹⁹ For I have chosen him, that he will command his children and his household after him to keep the way of the Lord by doing righteousness and justice, so that I[f] will bring about for him what I promised."

Abraham Pleads for the Righteous

²⁰ Then the Lord said, "The outcry of Sodom and Gomorrah is so great, and their sin is so exceedingly grave. ²¹ Now I am going down to see if what they have done is as bad as the outcry I hear. If not, I will know."

---

a   Genesis 18:10 reveals that one was God, and Genesis 19:10 reveals that the two others were angels.
b   Literally, "three seahs of grain." About 21 quarts.
c   Literally, "past the way of women."
d   Literally, "he."
e   Literally, "to send them."
f   Literally, "the Lord."

²² The *two angels in the form of* men started toward Sodom,ᵃ but Abraham remained standing before the Lᴏʀᴅ. ²³ Then Abraham approached him and asked, "Will you sweep away the righteous with the wicked? ²⁴ What if there are 50 righteous people in the city? Will you really sweep it away and not spare it for the sake of the 50 righteous people in it? ²⁵ Far be it from you to do such a thing—to kill the righteous with the wicked, to treat alike both the righteous and the wicked. Far be it from you! Will not the judge of all the earth do right?"

²⁶ The Lᴏʀᴅ said, "If I find 50 righteous people in Sodom, I will spare the whole place for their sake."ᵇ

²⁷ Then Abraham replied, "Now that I, though I am nothing but dust and ashes, have been so bold as to speak, ²⁸ what if there are 5 less than 50? Will you destroy the whole city because of 5?"

"If I find 45," he said, "I will not destroy it."

²⁹ Abraham spoke once again. "What if only 40 are found there?"

He said, "For the sake of 40, I will not do it."

³⁰ Then he said, "May the Lord not be angry, but let me speak. What if only 30 can be found there?"

He answered, "I will not do it if I find 30 there."

³¹ Abraham (thinking, "Since I have *already* risked speaking to the Lord") said, "What if only 20 can be found there?"

He said, "For the sake of 20, I will not destroy it."

³² Then he said, "Lord, don't be angry, but let me speak just one more time. What if only 10 can be found there?"

He answered, "For the sake of 10, I will not destroy it."

³³ When the Lᴏʀᴅ finished speaking with Abraham, he left, and Abraham returned to his place.

Genesis 19
Sodom and Gomorrah Destroyed

¹ The two angels *in the form of men* arrived at Sodom in the evening. Lot, sitting at the city gate, saw them and got up to meet them. He bowed with his face to the earth ² and said, "My Lords, please turn aside to your servant's house. Wash your feet, spend the night, and then go on your way in the morning."

"No," they answered, "we'll spend the night in the square."

³ But he insisted so strongly that they turned and entered his house. He prepared unleavened breadᶜ and a feast, and they ate.

⁴ Before they had gone to bed,ᵈ young and old men of Sodom from every part of the city surrounded the house. ⁵ They called to Lot, "Where are the men who came to you tonight? Bring them out so that we can have sex with them."

---

a Literally, "turned away and went toward Sodom."
b Or "on account of them." And occurrences in the next paragraph.
c "Unleavened": Made without yeast or any other leavening agent used to lighten or increase the volume of the dough.
d Literally, "lain down."

⁶ Lot went outside, shut the door behind him, ⁷ and said, "Please, my friends, don't do this wicked thing. ⁸ Look, I have two daughters who have not had sex with men. Please let me bring them out to you. Do whatever you like*a* with them. But don't do anything to these men. They have come under the protection of my roof."

⁹ "Stand aside," they replied. "You, the one who came to live *here* temporarily, want to play the judge! Now we'll treat you worse than them." Then they pressured the man Lot by moving forward to break down the door.

¹⁰ But the *angels* reached out and pulled Lot into the house and shut the door. ¹¹ Then they struck all the men, young an old, who were at the door of the house with blindness so that they grew weary trying to find the door. ¹² Then the two man-*like* *angels* asked, "Who else do you have here—sons, sons-in-law, or daughters? Everyone, whoever *belongs to you* in the city, get them out of here—¹³ because we are about to destroy this place! The outcry has become so great before the Lᴏʀᴅ that he has sent us to destroy it."

¹⁴ So Lot went out to his sons-in-law who were *pledged* to marry his daughters and said, "Get up! Get out of this place, because the Lᴏʀᴅ is about to destroy it!" But they thought he was joking.

¹⁵ At dawn, the angels urged Lot *again*, "Get up! Take your wife and your two daughters who are here, or you will be swept away when the city is punished." ¹⁶ Lot hesitated, so they grasped his hand and the hands of his wife and two daughters and took them out of the city, for the Lᴏʀᴅ was merciful to them. ¹⁷ As soon as they had brought them out, one of them said, "Flee for your lives! Don't look back, and don't stay anywhere in the valley. Escape to the mountains or you will be swept away!"

¹⁸ But Lot said to them, "Oh no, my lords! ¹⁹ Your servant has found favor in your sight, and you have shown lovingkindness to me by sparing my life. But I can't flee to the mountains. The disaster will overtake me, and I'll die. ²⁰ Look, here's a town near enough to flee to. It is small. Let me escape there and my life will be saved. It's just a small place."

²¹ The angel replied, "Very well, I'll grant you this request too. I will not overthrow the town of which you speak. ²² But hurry and escape to there, because I cannot do anything until you get there." Thus the town was called Zoar (*i.e.,* Little Place).

²³ By the time Lot reached Zoar, the sun had risen over the earth. ²⁴ Then the Lᴏʀᴅ rained fire and burning sulfur out of the heavens onto Sodom and Gomorrah. ²⁵ He overthrew the cities and all their inhabitants, *along with* the entire valley, and even the vegetation.*b* ²⁶ But Lot's wife looked *back* from behind him, and she became a pillar of salt.

²⁷ Early the next morning Abraham returned to where he had stood before the Lᴏʀᴅ. ²⁸ He looked down toward the valley of Sodom and Gomorrah and saw the smoke of the *burning* land rising like smoke from a furnace.

²⁹ And *that's how* it happened. When God destroyed the cities of the valley, when he overthrew the cities in which Lot had lived, he remembered Abraham and brought Lot out from the midst of the destruction.*c*

---

a Literally, "whatever is good in your eyes."

b Literally, "what grew on the ground."

c Literally, "the overthrow."

Moab and Ammon Born Out of Incest

³⁰ Lot and his two daughters left Zoar and lived in a cave in the mountains, for he was afraid to stay in Zoar. ³¹ One day the firstborn said to the younger, "Our father is old, and there's no man on earth here to marry us,ᵃ as is the custom everywhere on the earth. ³² Come, let's get our father to drink wine and lie with us so we can preserve our family line through him." ³³ That night they got him drunk, and the firstborn went in and had sex with him. He did not know when she lay down or when she got up.

³⁴ The next day she told her younger sister,ᵇ "Last night I had sex with Father. Let's get him drunk with wine again tonight. Then you go and have sex with him so we may preserve our family line through him." ³⁵ So they got him drunk with wine again, and she got up and had sex with him. And he did not know when she lay down or when she got up. ³⁶ So both of Lot's daughters became pregnant by their father. ³⁷ The firstborn had a son she named Moab (*i.e.*, From the Father). He is the father of today's Moabites. ³⁸ The younger one had a son she named Ben-Ammi (*i.e.,* Son of My People). He is the father of today's Ammonites.

Genesis 20
Abraham Calls Sarah His Sister

¹ Abraham moved to the Negev and settled between Kadesh and Shur, and he dwelled awhile in Gerar. ² *While there,* he said of Sarah his wife, "She is my sister. So Gerar's king, Abimelech, sent for Sarah and took her. ³ But God came to Abimelech in a dream one night and told him, "Behold, you are a dead man because of the woman you have taken, for she is married."

⁴ Now Abimelech had not gone near her, so he said, "Lord, will you destroy an innocent nation? ⁵ Didn't he himself say, 'She is my sister,' and she herself say, 'He is my brother'? I have done this with a clear conscienceᶜ and innocent hands."

⁶ In the dream God said, "Yes, I know that you have done this with a clear conscience, so I kept you from sinning against me. That's why I kept you from touching her. ⁷ Now return the man's wife, for he is a prophet. He will pray for you and you will live. But if you do not return her, you may be sure that you and all who are yours will surely die."

⁸ So Abimelech arose in the morning and summoned all his officialsᵈ and told them what had happened. Upon hearing this, they were quite afraid. ⁹ Then he called in Abraham and said, "What have you done to us? How have I sinned against you that you have brought such great sin upon me and my kingdom? You have done things to me that should not be done. ¹⁰ What did you see that *caused* you to do this?"

¹¹ Abraham replied, "Because I thought that there is no fear of God in this place and that you would kill me because of my wife. ¹² Besides, she really is my sister, the daughter of my father but not the daughter of my mother, and she became my

---

a Literally, "come in to us." Or "come *to bed* with us."
b Literally, "the firstborn told the younger."
c Literally, "in the integrity of my heart." And next sentence.
d Literally, "servants."

28

wife. ¹³ When God caused me to wander from my father's house, I suggested *to my wife,* 'This is how you can show your kindness to me: Everywhere we go, tell them that I am your brother.' "

¹⁴ Then Abimelech returned Abraham's wife Sarah and brought him sheep and oxen and male and female servants. ¹⁵ And he said, "Look, all my land is before you. Settle wherever you like." ¹⁶ And to Sarah he said, "Look, I am giving your brother twenty-five pounds of silver^a as a sign of your innocence^b to those who are with you.^{c} Before everyone, you are cleared.

¹⁷ Then Abraham prayed to God and God healed Abimelech, his wife, and his slave girls so they could bear children, ¹⁸ for the LORD had closed all the wombs in Abimelech's household because of Abraham's wife Sarah.

Genesis 21
Birth of Isaac. Hagar and Ishmael Sent Away

¹ Now the LORD visited Sarah as he had said, and he did for Sarah as he had promised. ⁵ When Abraham was one hundred years old, ² at the time God had promised,^{d} she conceived and bore him a son. ³ Abraham named him^e Isaac (*i.e.,* He Laughs). ⁴ And Abraham circumcised his son Isaac when he was eight days old, as God had commanded him.

⁶ Sarah said, "God has brought me laughter. Everyone who hears will laugh with me, ⁷ for who would have told Abraham that Sarah would nurse children? Yet I have borne him a son in his old age."

⁸ Isaac grew, and Abraham held a great feast on the day he was weaned.
⁹ But Sarah saw that *Ishmael* (whom Hagar the Egyptian had borne to Abraham) was making fun of Isaac, ¹⁰ so she told Abraham, "Get rid of that maidservant and her son, for I won't have the son of that slave woman as an heir with my son Isaac."^{f}

¹¹ The matter grieved Abraham greatly, because *Ishmael was* his son. ¹² But God said, "Do not grieve about the boy and your maidservant. Whatever Sarah tells you, do it,^{g} for your descendants will be named through Isaac. ¹³ I will make your son of the maidservant into a nation too, because he is your descendant." ¹⁴ So Abraham rose early in the morning and took bread and a skin of water and gave them to Hagar. He put them on her shoulder, *gave her* the boy, and sent her away. And she left and wandered about in the wilderness of Beersheba.

¹⁵ When the water in the skin was gone, she put Ishmael under a bush ¹⁶ and sat down opposite him, about a bowshot^h away, thinking, "I cannot watch the boy die." As she sat across from him, she lifted her voice, weeping. ¹⁷ God heard the boy crying, and the angel of God called to Hagar from heaven, "What is wrong, Hagar?

a   Literally, "a thousand shekels."
b   Literally, "your vindication."
c   Literally, "before all the eyes of those who are with you."
d   See Genesis 18:10.
e   Literally, "the son who was born to him, whom Sarah bore him."
f   Literally, "for the son of that slave woman shall not be an heir with my son Isaac."
g   Literally, "listen to her voice."
h   "Bowshot": about a hundred yards.

Do not be afraid. God has heard the boy crying.*ᵃ* ¹⁸ Get up, take the boy, and hold him by the hand, for I will make a great nation from him."

¹⁹ Then God opened her eyes and she saw a well. So she filled the skin with water and gave the boy a drink. ²⁰⁻²¹ God was with Ishmael as he grew up in the wilderness of Paran. He became an archer, and Hagar found a wife for him from Egypt.

Treaty with the Philistines

²² Then Abimelech and his army commander, Phicol, said to Abraham, "God is with you in all that you do. ²³ Now swear that you will not deal falsely with me or my children or my descendants and that *you will show* us the kindness that we have shown you in *our* country where you reside as a foreigner.

²⁴ Abraham said, "I swear it."

²⁵ Then Abraham complained to Abimelech about a well that Abimelech's servants had seized. ²⁶ Abimelech responded, "I don't know who did it. You didn't tell me, and I didn't hear of it until today." ²⁷ Then Abraham gave sheep and cattle to Abimelech, and the two *men* made a treaty. ²⁸ When Abraham set apart seven of his ewe lambs, ²⁹ Abimelech asked him, "What is the meaning of this?"*ᵇ*

³⁰ Abraham replied, "Take these seven ewe lambs from my hand as a witness that I dug this well." ³¹ So they swore an oath. ³² And because the two of them swore an oath there, he named the place Beersheba (*i.e.,* Well of the Oath). Then Abimelech and Phicol arose and returned to the land of the Philistines. ³³ Abraham planted a tamarisk tree at Beersheba, and he called upon the name of the Lord, the Eternal God. ³⁴ And he lived in the land of the Philistines for many days.

Genesis 22
God Asks Abraham to Sacrifice Isaac

¹ After these events, God tested Abraham. He called, "Abraham!"

"Here I am," Abraham replied.

² Then God said, "Take your son, your only son—Isaac, whom you love—and go to the land of Moriah.*ᶜ* Offer him there as a burnt offering on one of the mountains I tell you about."

³ So early in the morning Abraham arose, saddled his donkey, and took his son Isaac and two servants.*ᵈ* After he had cut wood for the burnt offering, he set out for the place God had told him about. ⁴ On the third day Abraham saw the place in the distance. ⁵ He said to the servants, "Stay here with the donkey while the boy and I go over there. We will worship and then return." ⁶ Abraham took the wood for the burnt offering and loaded it on Isaac. In his hands he carried the fire and the knife. And the two of them walked together.

⁷ Isaac said to his father, Abraham, "Father?"

"Yes, my son?" Abraham replied.

"Look, the fire and wood *are here*," Isaac said, "but where is the lamb for the

---

a   Literally, "the voice of the boy where he is."
b   Literally, "of these seven ewe lambs that you set apart."
c   "Moriah": the site of "Moriah" is unknown. See "Geography of Isaac" for more information.
d   Literally, "young men." And verse 5.

burnt offering?"

⁸ Abraham answered, "God himself will provide*a* the lamb for the burnt offering, my son." And the two of them went on together.

⁹ When they arrived at Mount Moriah,*b* Abraham built an altar, arranged the wood, bound his son Isaac, and laid him on the altar on top of the wood. ¹⁰ Then Abraham stretched out his hand and took the knife to slay his son. ¹¹ But the angel of the Lord called out to him from heaven, "Abraham! Abraham!"

"Here I am," Abraham replied.

¹² "Do not lay your hand against the boy," he said. "Do nothing to him. For now I know that you fear God, since you have not withheld from me your son, your only son."

¹³ Then Abraham saw a ram behind him caught by its horns in the thicket. He took the ram and sacrificed it as a burnt offering instead of his son. ¹⁴ Abraham called the name of that place Yahweh Yireh (*i.e.,* The Lord Will Provide), and it is still said, "On the mountain of the Lord it will be provided."

¹⁵ Then the angel of the Lord called to Abraham from heaven a second time ¹⁶ and said, "I myself swear, declares the Lord, that because you have done this and have not withheld your son, your only son, ¹⁷ I will certainly bless you, and I will multiply your descendants enormously—as the stars of the heavens and as the sand of the seashore. And your descendants will take possession of their enemies' cities.*c* ¹⁸ And through your descendants all the nations on earth will be blessed because you have obeyed my voice."

¹⁹ Then Abraham returned to his servants, and they returned to Beersheba. And Abraham lived there. ²⁰ Later Abraham was told, "Milcah has borne *eight* sons to your brother Nahor."

---

a   Or "God for himself will provide."
b   Literally, "at the place of which God had told him."
c   Literally, "take the gates of their enemies."

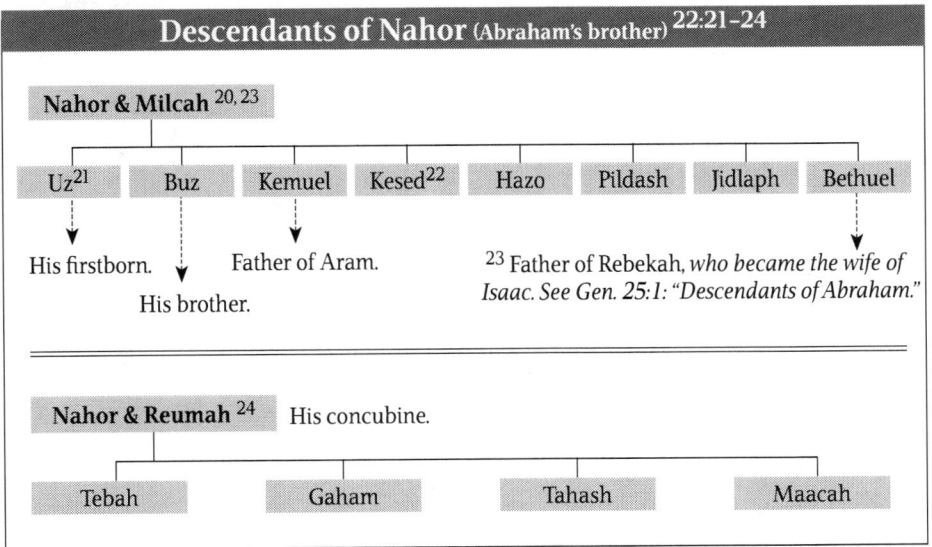

Descendants of Nahor (Abraham's brother) 22:21-24

Nahor & Milcah 20, 23

| Uz²¹ | Buz | Kemuel | Kesed²² | Hazo | Pildash | Jidlaph | Bethuel |

His firstborn.   Father of Aram.   ²³ Father of Rebekah, *who became the wife of*

His brother.   *Isaac. See Gen. 25:1: "Descendants of Abraham."*

Nahor & Reumah 24   His concubine.

| Tebah | Gaham | Tahash | Maacah |

Genesis 23
Death of Sarah

¹ Sarah lived 127 years.*ᵃ* ² She died in Kiriath Arba (*i.e.,* Hebron) in Canaan, and Abraham went in to mourn and weep for her. ³ Then he rose from beside his dead *wife* and said to the Hittites, ⁴ "I am a stranger living among you temporarily. Sell me a burial site so I can bury my dead out of my sight."

⁵ The Hittites replied, ⁶ "Hear us, my lord: You are a mighty prince among us. Bury your dead in the choicest of our tombs. None of us will refuse you his tomb for burying your dead."

⁷ Abraham got up, bowed before the people of the land, the Hittites, ⁸ and said, "If you are willing to let me bury my dead, then listen to me and intercede for me with Ephron, the son of Zohar, ⁹ so he will sell me the cave of Machpelah he owns. It's at the end of his field. Let him sell it to me in your presence for a burial site for the full price."

¹⁰ *Now* Ephron the Hittite was sitting among the Hittites. *So* he replied to Abraham within hearing of the *other* Hittites who had come to the gate of his city: ¹¹ "No, my lord. Listen to me. I give you the field and I give you the cave that is in it. I give it to you in the presence of my people. Bury your dead."

¹² Abraham bowed down before the people of the land and said, ¹³ "If you will, please listen. I will pay*ᵇ* for the field. Accept it from me so I may bury my dead there."

¹⁴ Ephron replied, ¹⁵"Listen to me, my lord. The land is worth nine pounds of silver,*ᶜ* but what is that between you and me? Bury your dead."

¹⁶ Abraham listened to Ephron and weighed out for him the silver that he had named within hearing of the Hittites—nine pounds of silver.*ᵈ*

¹⁷ Then Ephron's field in Machpelah (east of*ᵉ* Mamre), with the cave and all the trees in the field, were deeded ¹⁸ *to Abraham* in the presence of*ᶠ* all the Hittites who were at the city gate. ¹⁹ Then Abraham buried Sarah there in the cave in Canaan in the cave of the field of Machpelah, east of Mamre (i.e., Hebron) in Canaan. ²⁰ That is how the field and the cave that is in it were deeded to Abraham as a burial site by the Hittites.

Genesis 24
Servant Sent to Find Isaac a Wife

¹ Now Abraham was very old,*ᵍ* and the Lᴏʀᴅ had blessed him in every way. ² He said to his oldest household servant, who had charge of all that he had,*ʰ* "Put your hand under my thigh. ³ Swear *an oath* by the Lᴏʀᴅ, the God of heaven and the God

---

a Literally, "Sarah lived 127 years. These were the years of the life of Sarah."
b Literally, "give the price."
c Literally, "four hundred shekels of silver."
d Literally, "four hundred shekels of silver according to the measures used among the merchants."
e Or "facing."
f Literally, "before."
g Literally, "very old and advanced in years."
h Genesis 15:2 provides an indication that this was Eliezer.

of earth, that you will not get a wife for Isaac from the daughters of the Canaanites among whom I live, ⁴ but will go to my country and my relatives and get a wife for him."

⁵ The servant asked, "What if the woman does not want to come to this land? Should I take Isaac back to the land from which you came?"

⁶ Abraham replied, "Be careful not to take my son back there. ⁷ The LORD, the God of heaven, who brought me out of my father's house and my native land, swore, 'I will give this land to your descendants.' He will send his angel before you, and you will get a wife for my son from there. ⁸ If the woman is unwilling to follow you, you will be free from this oath. Just don't take my son back there."

⁹ So the servant put his hand under Abraham's thigh and swore concerning the matter.

¹⁰ The servant took ten of Abraham's camels and all kinds of good things and left for *the city where* Nahor *lived* in Aram *in* Naharaim (*i.e.*, Two Rivers).

Toward evening, when women draw water, ¹¹ he had the camels kneel down near the well outside the town. ¹² Then he prayed, "O LORD, God of my master Abraham, now*ᵃ* grant me success today, and show lovingkindness to my master Abraham. ¹³ Here I am standing by this spring, and the women*ᵇ* are coming out to draw water. ¹⁴ Now when I say, 'Please let down your jar so I can have a drink,' may it be that the girl who answers, 'Drink, and I'll water your camels also,' *is the one* you have chosen for your servant Isaac. This way I will know that you have shown lovingkindness to my master."

¹⁵ Before he had finished speaking, Rebekah*ᶜ* came out with her jar on her shoulder. ¹⁶ She looked very beautiful and was a virgin.*ᵈ* She went down to the spring, filled her jar, and came back.

¹⁷ Then the servant ran to meet her and said, "Please give me a little drink of water from your jar."

¹⁸ She replied, "Drink, my lord," and quickly lowered the jar*ᵉ* and gave him a drink.

¹⁹ When she finished giving him a drink, she said, "I'll draw water for your camels too, until they have finished drinking." ²⁰ And she quickly emptied her jar into the trough and ran back to the well to draw water*ᶠ* for all his camels. ²¹ In silence, the man watched her to know whether or not the LORD had made his journey successful.

²² When the camels had finished drinking, the man took out a gold nose ring weighing one-sixth of an ounce*ᵍ* and two gold wrist bracelets that weighed almost four ounces,*ʰ* ²³ and said, "Whose daughter are you? Please tell me. Is there room for us to stay in your father's house?"

²⁴ She replied, "I am the daughter of Bethuel, the granddaughter of Milcah and Nahor.*ⁱ* ²⁵ We have plenty of straw and feed, as well as room for you to spend the night."

---

a   Or "please."
b   Literally, "daughters of the men."
c   Literally, "Rebekah, the daughter of Bethuel (the son of Abraham's brother Nahor and his wife, Milcah)."
d   Literally, "and no man had had sex with her."
e   Literally, "lowered the jar in her hands."
f   Literally, "to draw water, and she drew water."
g   Literally, "weighing half of a shekel.
h   Literally, "ten *shekels*."
i   Literally, "Nahor's son, whom Milcah bore to him."

²⁶ Then the man bowed and worshiped the LORD ²⁷ and said, "Blessed be*a* the LORD, the God of my master Abraham, who has not forsaken his lovingkindness and his faithfulness toward my master. As for me, the LORD has guided me on the journey to the house of my master's kin." ²⁸ Then the girl ran and told her mother's household about these things.

²⁹ Rebekah's brother, Laban,*b* ran to Abraham's servant*c* at the spring. ³⁰ When Laban saw the nose ring and bracelets and heard what the man had said to her,*d* he went to the man (who was still standing by the camels at the spring) ³¹ and said, "Come. You are blessed of the LORD. Why are you standing outside, for I have prepared the house and a place for the camels."

³² So the man went to the house, unloaded the camels, and fed them grain and fodder. And *Laban provided* water for him and his men to wash their feet.

³³ When food was set before them to eat, the servant said, "I will not eat until I have told you my business."*e*

Laban replied, "Tell us."

³⁴ And he told them: "I am Abraham's servant. ³⁵ The LORD has blessed my master, and he has become wealthy.*f* He has given him sheep and cattle, silver and gold, menservants and maidservants, and camels and donkeys. ³⁶ Sarah, my master's wife, bore him a son in her old age, and he has given him everything he has. ³⁷ Abraham made me swear an oath, explaining 'You will not get a wife for Isaac from the daughters of the Canaanites in whose land I live, ³⁸ but will go to my father's house and my relatives to get a wife for him.'

³⁹ I asked my master, 'Suppose the woman will not come back with me?'

⁴⁰ He said, 'The LORD, before whom I have walked, will send his angel and make your journey successful so that you can get a wife for my son from my father's clan and household. ⁴¹ You will be free from my oath if, when you get to my clan, they do not give her to you. You will be released from my oath.'

⁴² "So today I came to the spring and prayed, 'O LORD, God of my master Abraham, please make this journey I have come on successful. ⁴³ Look, I'm standing by this spring. If I say, "Please let me drink a little water from your jar" to a young woman*g* who comes out to draw water ⁴⁴ and she replies, "Drink, and I'll draw water for your camels also," let her be the woman whom the LORD has chosen for Isaac.'

⁴² "Before I finished thinking in my heart, guess what—Rebekah came out with her jar on her shoulder and went to the spring and drew water! I said to her, 'Please give me a drink.' ⁴⁶ She quickly lowered her jar from her shoulder and said, 'Drink, and I'll water your camels also.' So I drank, and she watered the camels too.

⁴⁷ "Then I asked, 'Whose daughter are you?' She said, 'I'm the daughter of Bethuel,

---

a   Or "praise be."
b   Literally, "Rebekah had a brother named Laban."
c   Literally, "ran to the man."
d   Literally, "and heard the words of Rebekah, his sister: 'this is what the man said to me.'"
e   Literally, "said what I have to say."
f   Literally, "blessed my master greatly, and he has become great."
g   Hebrew: *almah*, which refers to a young woman, a person who in that time was presumed to be a virgin.

the granddaughter of Milcah and Nahor."[a] So I put the ring in her nose and the bracelets on her wrists. [48] Then I bowed down and worshiped the LORD. I praised[b] the LORD, the God of my master Abraham, who had led me on the right road to get the granddaughter of my master's brother for his son. [49] So now if you will deal kindly and faithfully with my master, tell me. And if not, tell me, so I'll know which way to turn."[c]

[50] Laban and Bethuel replied, "Your words have come from the LORD; we cannot say *anything* for or against what you ask.[d] [51] Here's Rebekah. Take her and go. Let her become the wife of your master's son, as the LORD has spoken."

[52] When Abraham's servant heard their words, he bowed down to the ground before the LORD. [53] Then the servant brought out gold and silver jewelry and garments and gave them to Rebekah. He also gave precious gifts to her brother and mother. [54] Then he and the men with him ate and drank and spent the night there.

When they got up in the morning, he said, "Send me on my way to my master."

[55] But her brother and her mother said, "Let the young girl stay with us ten days *or so.* Then she may go."

[56] He replied, "Don't delay me, since the LORD has granted success to my journey. Send me on my way so that I may go to my master."

[57] They said, "Let's call Rebekah and ask for her answer."[e] [58] Then they called her and asked, "Will you go with this man?"

She said, "I will go."

[59] So they sent their sister Rebekah and her nurse[f] with Abraham's servant and his men. [60] And they blessed Rebekah: "May you, our sister, become thousands upon thousands. May your descendants control the city gates[g] of their enemies."

[61] Then Rebekah and her maidservants arose, mounted the camels, and followed the man. So the servant took Rebekah and departed.

Isaac Marries Rebekah

[62] One evening, Isaac (who was living in the Negev and had *just* come from Beer Lahai Roi) [53] went out to a field to meditate, and he saw camels approaching. [54] Rebekah saw Isaac, got off her camel, [55] and asked the servant, "Who is that man in the field walking to meet us?"

The servant answered, "It's my master." So she took her veil and covered herself.

[66] Then the servant told Isaac everything that he had done. [67] Isaac brought Rebekah into his mother Sarah's tent and married her. So she became his wife, and he fell in love with her.[h] Thus Isaac was comforted after his mother's death.

---

a   Literally, "Nahor's son, whom Milcah bore to him."
b   Or "blessed be."
c   Literally, "whether to turn to the right or to the left."
d   Literally, "cannot say good or bad."
e   Literally, "consult her mouth."
f   "Nurse": a woman who suckles a very young child and helps raise the child.
g   Literally, "possess the gate."
h   Literally, "loved her."

Genesis 25

Descendants of Abraham Gen. 25:1–4, 12–20, 25–26

[19] This is the family history of Isaac.

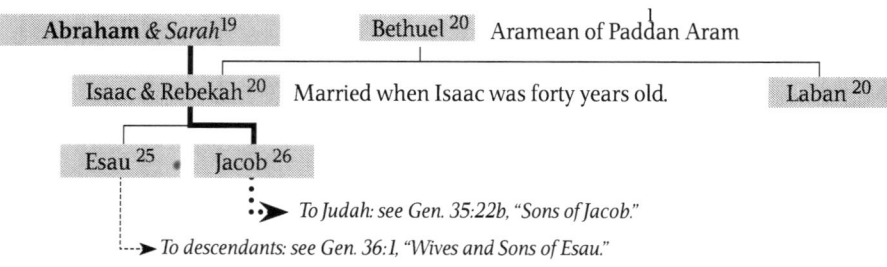

- Abraham & Sarah[19]
- Bethuel [20] Aramean of Paddan Aram
- Isaac & Rebekah [20] Married when Isaac was forty years old.
- Laban [20]
- Esau [25] Jacob [26]
  - To Judah: see Gen. 35:22b, "Sons of Jacob."
  - To descendants: see Gen. 36:1, "Wives and Sons of Esau."

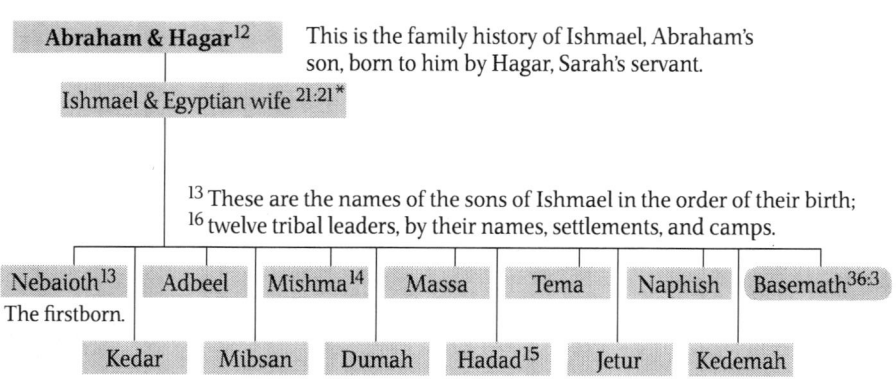

- Abraham & Hagar[12] This is the family history of Ishmael, Abraham's son, born to him by Hagar, Sarah's servant.
- Ishmael & Egyptian wife [21:21]*

[13] These are the names of the sons of Ishmael in the order of their birth; [16] twelve tribal leaders, by their names, settlements, and camps.

Nebaioth[13] The firstborn.	Adbeel	Mishma[14]	Massa	Tema	Naphish	Basemath[36:3]
	Kedar	Mibsan	Dumah	Hadad[15]	Jetur	Kedemah

*[17] Ishmael lived 137 years. He breathed *his last* and died and was gathered to his people. [18] His sons[a] settled from Havilah to Shur, on the land east of Egypt,[b] toward Ashur.[c] They settled there in defiance of[d] all their relatives.

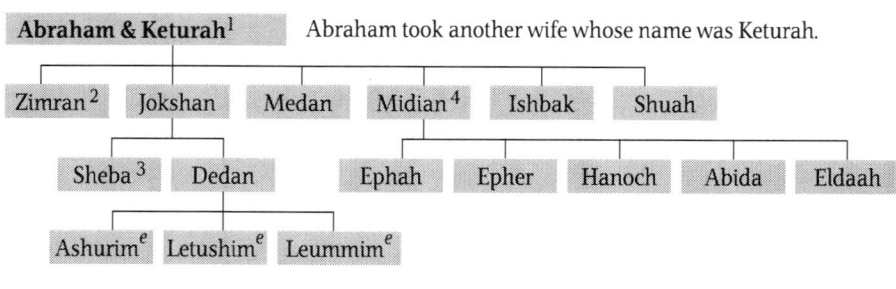

- Abraham & Keturah[1] Abraham took another wife whose name was Keturah.

Zimran [2]	Jokshan	Medan	Midian [4]	Ishbak	Shuah
	Sheba [3] Dedan		Ephah Epher Hanoch Abida Eldaah		
Ashurim[e] Letushim[e] Leummim[e]					

a Literally, "they."

b Literally, "before Egypt."

c "Ashur": a city on the west bank of the Tigris Riever, north of Babylon and south of Nineveh.

d Literally, "on the face of."

e Or "the Ashurites, Letushites, and Leummites."

Abraham Dies. Esau and Jacob Born

⁶ While he was still living, Abraham gave gifts to the sons of his concubines and sent them to the east,*ᵃ* away from his son Isaac. ⁵ He left everything *else* he owned to Isaac. ⁷ Abraham lived 175 years. ⁸ Then, an old man full of years, he breathed his last, died at a ripe old age, and was gathered to his people. ⁹⁻¹⁰ His sons Isaac and Ishmael buried him with his wife Sarah in the cave of Machpelah near Mamre, in the field of Ephron, son of Zohar the Hittite—the field Abraham purchased from the Hittites. ¹¹ After Abraham's death, God blessed his son Isaac. And Isaac settled near Beer Lahai Roi.

²⁰ When Isaac was forty years old, he married Rebekah. ²¹ He prayed to the LORD on behalf of his wife because she was barren. The LORD answered his prayer, and she conceived. ²² But the babies clashed inside her, and she wondered, "Why is this happening?" ²³ So she asked the LORD.

He replied, "Two nations are in your womb, and the two peoples *who will come* from within you will be divided. One will be stronger than the other, and the older will serve the younger."

²⁴ At birth,*ᵇ* indeed, there were twins in her womb. ²⁵ The first came out red, hairy all over like a garment. So they named him Esau (*i.e.,* Hairy). ²⁶ Afterward, his brother came out with his hand holding Esau's heel; so he was named Jacob (*i.e.,* He Grasps). Isaac was sixty years old when Rebekah bore them. ²⁷ When the boys grew up, Esau became a skillful hunter, an outdoorsman. But Jacob was a quiet man, staying among the tents.

Esau Sells His Inheritance

²⁸ Now Isaac, with his taste for wild game, loved Esau, but Rebekah loved Jacob. ²⁹ *One day when* Jacob had cooked stew, Esau came in from the fields and he was famished. ³⁰ He said "Please, let me have some of that red stew. I'm famished. (That is why he was *also* called Edom.*ᶜ*)

³¹ Jacob replied, "First sell me your birthright."*ᵈ*

³² And Esau said, "Look at me! I'm about to die! What use is a birthright?"

³³ So Jacob said, "Swear to me first."

So Esau swore an oath, selling his birthright to Jacob. ³⁴ Then Jacob gave Esau some bread and lentil stew. He ate and drank, then rose and left. Thus Esau despised*ᵉ* his birthright.

Genesis 26
Abrahamic Covenant Reaffirmed to Isaac

¹ Now there was a famine in the land, besides the former famine of Abraham's time. So Isaac went to Abimelech, king of the Philistines in Gerar. ² The LORD appeared

---

a Literally, "east, to the land of the east."

b Literally, "when her days were fulfilled."

c Perhaps a wordplay on the figurative meaning of "red" (the meaning of "Edom"), implying impulsiveness.

d "Birthright": rights normally granted by birth to the first born son (e.g., family name, titles, and possessions) but not received until the death of the preceding person with the birthright.

e "Despise": express an attitude of hatred or disgust toward something because it is seen as worthless or undeserving of respect.

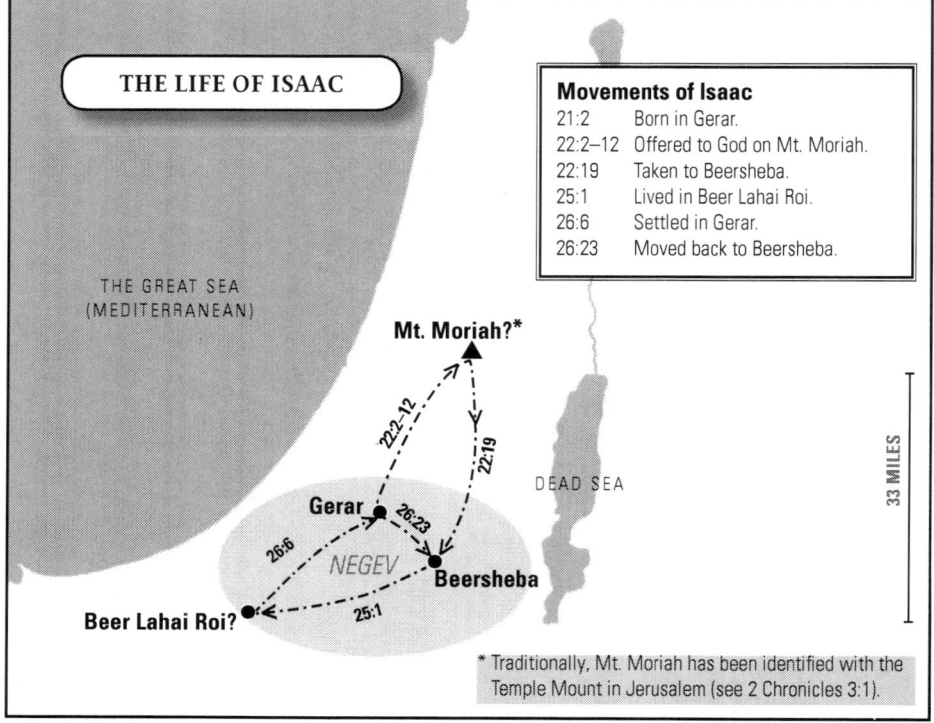

THE LIFE OF ISAAC

Movements of Isaac

21:2	Born in Gerar.
22:2–12	Offered to God on Mt. Moriah.
22:19	Taken to Beersheba.
25:1	Lived in Beer Lahai Roi.
26:6	Settled in Gerar.
26:23	Moved back to Beersheba.

THE GREAT SEA
(MEDITERRANEAN)

Mt. Moriah?*

DEAD SEA

33 MILES

Gerar

NEGEV

Beersheba

Beer Lahai Roi?

* Traditionally, Mt. Moriah has been identified with the
Temple Mount in Jerusalem (see 2 Chronicles 3:1).

to Isaac and said, "Do not go down to Egypt. ³ Settle in the land I will tell you about. Live as resident foreigners in this land, and I will be with you and will bless you. ⁴ For to you and your descendants

- I will give all these lands;
- I will establish the oath I swore to your father, Abraham; and
- I will make your descendants as numerous as the stars of heaven.

⁵ I will give them all these lands, and through your descendants all nations on earth will be blessed because Abraham obeyed me and kept my charge, my commandments,[a] my rules, and my regulations." ⁶ So Isaac stayed in Gerar.

Isaac Calls Rebekah His Sister

⁷ When the men of Gerar asked about his wife, he said, "She is my sister." He was afraid to say "my wife," thinking,[b] "They might kill me because Rebekah is *so* beautiful."

⁸ When Isaac had been there a long time, Abimelech, king of the Philistines, looked out of a window and saw Isaac caressing Rebekah. ⁹ He summoned Isaac and said, "She is your wife! Why did you say, 'She is my sister'?"

Isaac replied, "Because I thought I might be killed on account of her."

---

a Or "commands."

b Literally, "otherwise."

¹⁰ Then Abimelech said, "What is this you have done to us? Someone might well have slept with your wife, and you would have brought guilt upon us." ¹¹ So Abimelech proclaimed:*ᵃ* "Anyone who touches this man or his wife must surely be put to death."

¹² That year Isaac planted crops in that land and reaped a hundredfold. ¹³ The Lord blessed him, and he became rich. ¹⁴ *His wealth* grew and grew until he became very wealthy *with* so many possessions—flocks and herds and servants—that the Philistines envied him. ¹⁵ So the Philistines filled with earth all the wells that his father Abraham's servants had dug in the days of Abraham.

¹⁶ Then Abimelech told Isaac, "Go away; you are too powerful for us." ¹⁷ So Isaac left and settled in the Valley of Gerar. ¹⁸ He *re*-dug the wells that had been dug in the days of his father, Abraham, which the Philistines had stopped up after he died. And he gave them the same names his father had given them.

¹⁹ When Isaac's servants dug in the Gerar valley and found a well of fresh*ᵇ* water, ²⁰ the herdsmen of Gerar quarreled with Isaac's herdsmen claiming, "The water is ours!" So Isaac named the well Esek (*i.e.,* Dispute) because they contended with him.

²¹ Then they dug another well, but they quarreled over it also. So he named it Sitnah (*i.e.,* Opposition). Then they moved on and dug another well, and *the herdsmen* did not quarrel over it. So he named it Rehoboth (*i.e.,* Broad Place), saying, "At last the Lord made room for us, and we will flourish in the land."

God Promises to Bless Isaac

²³ From there Isaac went up to Beersheba, ²⁴ and that night the Lord appeared to him and said, "I am the God of your father, Abraham. Do not be afraid, for I am with you. I will bless you and will multiply the number of your descendants for the sake of my servant Abraham." ²⁵ So Isaac built an altar there and called upon the name of the Lord.*ᶜ* Then he pitched his tent, and there his servants dug a well.

²⁶ One day Abimelech came from Gerar with his advisor, Ahuzzath, and the commander of his army, Phicol. ²⁷ Isaac asked, "Why have you come? You used to be hostile to me, and you sent me away."

²⁸ They said, "We see clearly that the Lord has been with you. So, we thought, there ought to be a pact between us, between you and us. Let's make a treaty ²⁹ that you will do us no harm, just as we did not touch you but treated you well and sent you away in peace. Now you are blessed by the Lord.

³⁰ Isaac prepared a feast, and they ate and drank together. ³¹ Early the next morning they exchanged oaths. Then Isaac sent them away, and they left in peace.

³² Later that day Isaac's servants told him about the well they had dug, saying, "We've found water!" ³³ He called it Shibah (*i.e.,* Oath). To this day the name of the town has been Beersheba (*i.e.,* Well of the Oath).

³⁴ When Esau was forty years old, he married *two women*: Judith (daughter of Beeri the Hittite) and Basemath (daughter of Elon the Hittite). ³⁵ They brought grief to Isaac and Rebekah.

---

a Literally, "ordered all the people."
b Or "flowing"; or "living."
c Literally, "called on the name of the Lord."

Genesis 27
Jacob Steals Esau's Blessing

¹ When Isaac was old and becoming blind,ᵃ he called for his older son Esau, saying, "My son."

"Here I am," he answered.

² Isaac said, "Look, I am an old man and don't know the day of my death. ³ Now then, get your weapons, your quiver and bow, and go to the fields and hunt some wild game for me. ⁴ Prepare some tasty dish I like and bring it to me to eat so that Iᵇ may bless you before I die."

⁵ But Rebekah was listening as Isaac spoke to Esau. So when Esau left for the fields to hunt game to bring Isaac, ⁶ she said to Jacob, "Look, I overheard your father tell Esau, ⁷ 'Bring me some game and prepare a tasty dish for me to eat. Then I will bless you in the presence of the LORD before I die.' ⁸ Now, my son, listen to my voice as I instruct you.ᶜ ⁹ Go to the flock and bring me two choice young goats so I can prepare a tasty dish for your father, just what he loves. ¹⁰ Then you will take it to him to eat so that he will bless you before he dies."

¹¹ Jacob objected, "But my brother Esau is a hairy man, and my skin is smooth.ᵈ ¹² What if my father feels me? He will see me as a deceiverᵉ and will put a curse upon me, not a blessing."

¹³ His mother said, "My son, let the curse be on me. Just do what I say. Go and get the goats for me."

¹⁴ So he got them and brought them to his mother, and she prepared some delicious food, just what his father loved. ¹⁵ Then Rebekah took Esau's best clothes (which she had in the house) and put them on Jacob. ¹⁶ She also covered his hands and the smooth part of his neck with the skin of the young goats. ¹⁷ Then she gave Jacob the tasty food and the bread she had made.

¹⁸ He went to his father and said, "My father."

And he responded, "Here I am. Who are you, my son?"

¹⁹ Jacob replied, "It's Esau, your firstborn. I have done as you told me. Please sit up and eat my game so that youᶠ may give me your blessing."

²⁰ But Isaac asked, "How could you get it so quickly, my son?"

And he replied, "Because the LORD your God caused it to happen."

²¹ Then Isaac said, "Come close so I can touch you, my son, to know whether you really are Esau or not." ²² Jacob went close, and Isaac touched him and said, "The voice is the voice of Jacob, but the hands are the hands of Esau." ²³ He did not recognize him because his hands were hairy like Esau's. So Isaac, *about* to bless him, ²⁴ asked, "Are you really my son Esau?"

"I am," he replied.

²⁵ Then Isaac said, "Bring *the food* to me to eat so I can eat my son's game and bless you."

---

a Literally, "his eyes were so dim that he could not see."
b Or "my soul."
c Literally, "command you."
d Literally, "and I am smooth."
e Literally, "I will become a deceiver in his sight."
f Or "your soul."

So Jacob brought it to him and he ate. He also brought him wine, and he drank. [26] Then his father Isaac said, "Come here and kiss me, my son." [27] So he went to him and kissed him. When Isaac smelled the smell of his clothes, he blessed him, saying, "Ah, the smell of my son is like the smell of a field that the LORD has blessed.

- [28] May God give you the dew of heaven and the riches*[a]* of the earth, an abundance of grain and new wine.

- [29] May nations serve you and peoples bow down to you.

- May you be master*[b]* over your brothers, and

- May the sons of your mother bow down to you.

- May those who curse you be cursed, and those who bless you be blessed."

Isaac's Prophecy About Esau

[30] As soon as Isaac finished blessing Jacob, right after Jacob had left his presence, Esau returned from hunting. [31] He too had prepared some tasty food. He brought it to his father and said, "My father, sit up and eat some of your son's game, that you*[c]* may bless me."

[32] Isaac replied, "Who are you?"

And he said, "I am your son, your firstborn, Esau."

[33] Isaac trembled and said, "Then who was it that hunted game and brought it to me? I ate it just before you came, and I blessed him—and indeed, he will be blessed!"

[34] When Esau heard his father's words, he cried out loudly and bitterly, "Bless me, me too, my father!"

[35] But Isaac replied, "Your brother came deceitfully and took your blessing."

[36] Esau said, "No wonder he's named Jacob.*[d]* He's tricked me twice: He took my birthright, and now he's taken my blessing! Haven't you reserved any blessing for me?"

[37] Isaac answered, "I have made him your master and have made all his relatives his servants, and I have provisioned*[e]* him with the grain and new wine. So what then can I do for you, my son?"

[38] Esau asked, "Do you have only one blessing, my father? Bless me also, my father!" Then he lifted his voice and wept.

[39] But Isaac said, "Your dwelling will be away from the earth's richness, away from the dew of heaven above. [40] You will live by the sword, and you will serve your brother. But when you grow restless, you will throw his yoke from your neck."

[41] Esau held a grudge against Jacob because of the blessing his father had given him. He schemed,*[f]* "The days of mourning for my father are near. *After them* I'll kill Jacob."

[42] When what Esau had said was reported to Rebekah, she sent for Jacob and told him, "Look, Esau is consoling himself *by planning* to kill you. [43] Now my son,

---

a   Literally, "fatness."

b   Or "lord."

c   Literally, "your soul."

d   Literally, "Isn't he rightly named Jacob," or, "Isn't he rightly named He Grasps."

e   Literally, "sustained."

f   Literally, "said to himself."

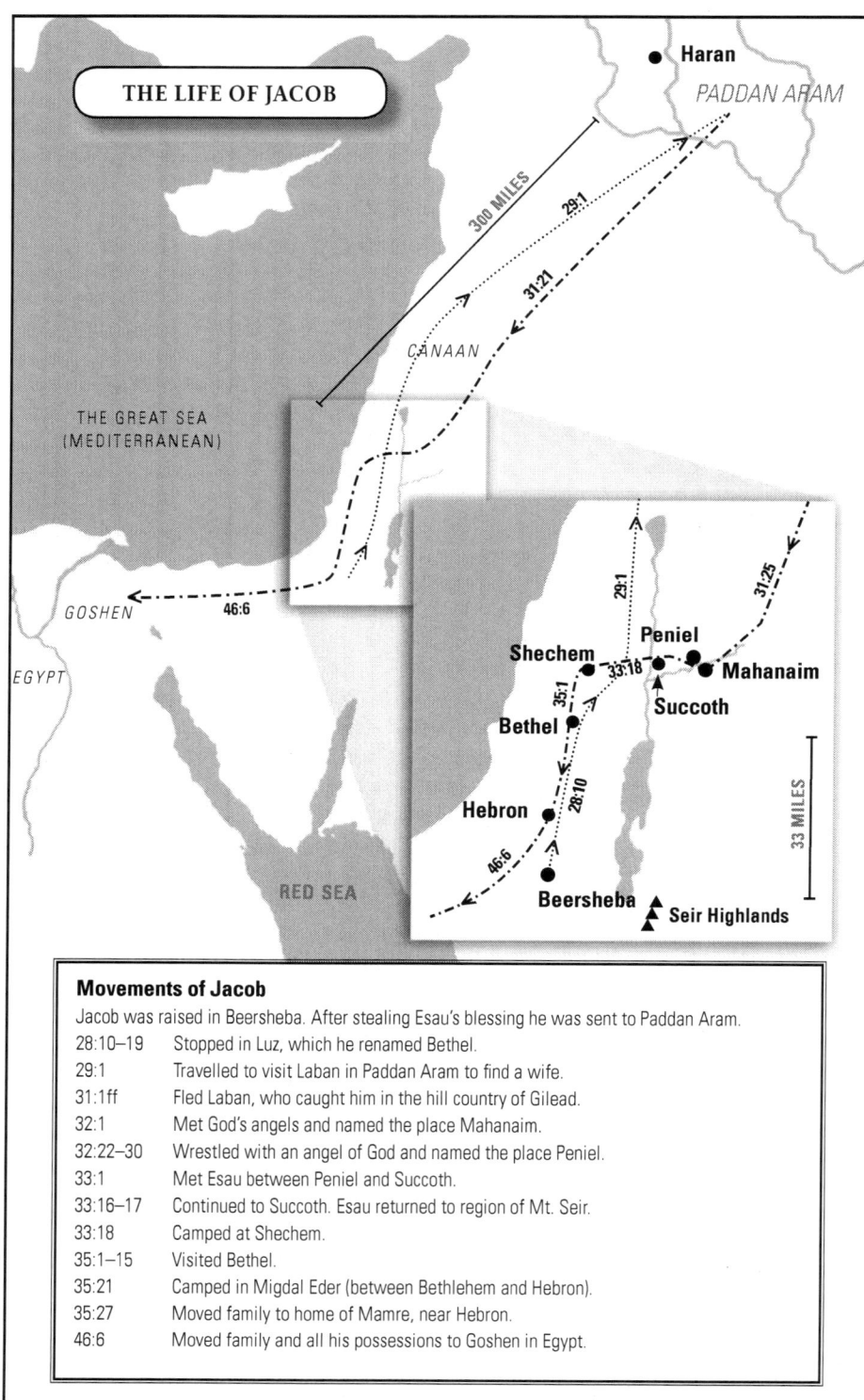

THE LIFE OF JACOB

Haran

PADDAN ARAM

300 MILES

29:1

31:21

CANAAN

THE GREAT SEA
(MEDITERRANEAN)

GOSHEN   46:6

EGYPT

RED SEA

Shechem   Peniel
33:18   Mahanaim

35:1   Succoth

Bethel

28:10

Hebron

46:6

33 MILES

Beersheba   Seir Highlands

29:1

31:25

Movements of Jacob

Jacob was raised in Beersheba. After stealing Esau's blessing he was sent to Paddan Aram.

28:10–19	Stopped in Luz, which he renamed Bethel.
29:1	Travelled to visit Laban in Paddan Aram to find a wife.
31:1ff	Fled Laban, who caught him in the hill country of Gilead.
32:1	Met God's angels and named the place Mahanaim.
32:22–30	Wrestled with an angel of God and named the place Peniel.
33:1	Met Esau between Peniel and Succoth.
33:16–17	Continued to Succoth. Esau returned to region of Mt. Seir.
33:18	Camped at Shechem.
35:1–15	Visited Bethel.
35:21	Camped in Migdal Eder (between Bethlehem and Hebron).
35:27	Moved family to home of Mamre, near Hebron.
46:6	Moved family and all his possessions to Goshen in Egypt.

obey my voice and flee to my brother Laban in Haran. Stay with him a few days [45] until your brother's fury subsides. When it does and he forgets what you did to him, I'll send *word* to get you back[a] from there. Why should I lose you both in one day?" [46]Then Rebekah told Isaac, "I'm tired of living because of these Hittite women.[b] If Jacob marries one of these local Hittite women,[c] what good will my life be to me?"

Genesis 28
Jacob Sent to Laban

[1] So Isaac called Jacob and blessed him and laid this charge on him: "Do not marry a Canaanite.[d] [2] Go now to Paddan Aram (*i.e.,* the fields of Aram), to the house of your mother's father, Bethuel. Take a wife there from among the daughters of Laban, your mother's brother. [3] May God Almighty bless you and make you fruitful and multiply you until you become a group of tribes.[e] [4] May he give you and your descendants the blessing of Abraham, that you may possess the land which God gave to Abraham where you *currently* live as a foreigner."

[5] Thus Isaac sent Jacob away, and he went to Laban (the son of Bethuel the Aramean, the brother of Rebekah, Esau and Jacob's mother) in Paddan Aram.

[6-9] Esau learned that Isaac had blessed Jacob, ordered him not to take a Canaanite wife, and sent him to Paddan Aram to take a wife from there. [7-8] And *he learned that*, in obedience to his father and mother, Jacob had gone to Paddan Aram. Esau then realized that Canaanite women displeased his father, [9] so he went to *the descendants of his uncle* Ishmael (Abraham's son) and married Mahalath[f] (the sister of Nebaioth and daughter of Ishmael) in addition to his *two Hittite* wives.

Jacob's Dream
Abrahamic Covenant Reaffirmed to Jacob

[10] Jacob left Beersheba and went toward Haran. [11] He reached Luz[g] and passed the night there because the sun had set. He took a stone, put it under his head, and lay down. [12] Then he had a dream:

> A ladder was standing on the earth reaching to heaven, and the angels of God were ascending and descending on it. [13] The LORD stood above it and said, "I am the LORD, the God of your father Abraham and the God of Isaac. I will give you and your descendants the land on which you lie. [14] Your descendants will be like the dust of the earth, and you will spread out to the north, east, south, and west. All peoples on earth will be blessed through you and your offspring. [15] I am with you and will watch over you wherever you go and will bring you back to this land. I will not leave you until I have done what I have promised you."

---

a   Literally, "to bring you from."
b   Perhaps a reference to Esau's two Hittite wives. See Genesis 26:34.
c   Literally, "daughters of Heth, daughters such as these, daughters of the land."
d   Literally, "from the daughters of Canaan."
e   Literally, "a company of peoples."
f   Or "Basemath." See Genesis 36:3.
g   Literally, "a certain place." Verse 19 tells us it was Luz, a place where Canaanites worshiped their gods.

16 When Jacob woke up, he thought, "Surely the LORD is in this place, and I didn't know it!" 17 He was afraid and said, "What an awesome place this is! This is none other than the house of God—the gate of heaven!" 18 Early in the morning Jacob took the stone he had put under his head and set it up as a *memorial* pillar and poured oil on top of it. 19 He called the place, a town that previously had been called Luz, Bethel (*i.e.,* House of God).

20 Then Jacob vowed, "If God will be with me and watch over me on this journey, will give me food to eat and clothes to wear 21 and return *me* safely to my father's house, then the LORD will be my God. 22 The stone that I have set up as a *memorial* pillar will be God's house,*a* and of all that he gives me I will give him a tenth."

Genesis 29
Jacob Marries Leah and Rachel

1 Jacob continued his journey and came to the land of the eastern people, *Paddan Aram.* 2 There he saw a well in a field with three flocks of sheep lying beside it (because the flocks were watered from the well). A large stone covered the mouth of the well. 3 When all the flocks were gathered, *the shepherds* would roll the stone from the well's mouth and water the sheep. Then they would put it back.*b*

4 Jacob asked *the shepherds,* "My brothers, where are you from?"

And they replied, "We're from Haran."

5 He asked, "Do you know Laban, Nahor's grandson?"

They replied, "We know him."

6 So he asked, "Is he well?"

And they replied, "He is well. Here comes his daughter Rachel with the sheep."

7 Jacob then said, "Look, the sun is still high. Isn't it time to gather the flocks? *Why don't you* water them and take them back to pasture."

9 But they replied, "We can't *water* them until all the flocks are gathered. Then we'll roll the stone away from the mouth of the well and water the sheep."

9 While he was still talking, Rachel, a shepherdess, came with her father Laban's sheep. 10 When Jacob saw her*c* and Laban's sheep, he went over and rolled the stone away and watered his uncle's flock. 11 Then he kissed Rachel and wept aloud. 12 He told her that he was a relative of her father, a son of Rebekah.

So she ran and told her father. 13 When Laban heard the news of Jacob, his sister's son, he ran to meet him, embraced him, kissed him, and brought him home. There Jacob told him his story.*d*

14 Then Laban said, "Surely you are my bone and my flesh." And Jacob stayed with them for a month.

15 *One day* Laban said, "Should you work for nothing just because you're a relative? What should your wages be?"

16 Now Laban had two daughters; the older was named Leah, and the younger,

---

a "God's house": a figurative term for a place of worship.
b Literally, "back on the mouth of the well."
c Literally, "saw Rachel, the daughter of Laban, his mother's brother."
d Literally, "all these things."

Rachel. Leah had weak eyes, but Rachel had a beautiful form and face. Jacob, who loved Rachel, said, "I'll work for you for seven years for your younger daughter Rachel."

¹⁹ Laban said, "It's better that I give her to you than to some other man. Stay here with us." ²⁰ So Jacob served seven years for Rachel, and they seemed but a few days to him because of his love for her.

²¹ *Seven years later* Jacob said to Laban, "My time is completed. Give me my wife so I may sleep with her." ²² So Laban gathered all the people of the place and celebrated with a feast.*ᵃ* ²³ But when evening came, he brought Leah to Jacob, and Jacob slept with her. ²⁴ Laban also gave his servant Zilpah to Leah as her maidservant.

²⁵ In the morning—surprise, it was Leah! So Jacob said to Laban, "What have you done to me? Didn't I serve you for Rachel? Why have you deceived me?"

²⁶ Laban replied, "It's not our custom*ᵇ* to marry off the younger daughter before the firstborn. ²⁷ Finish Leah's *bridal* week. Then we will give you the younger one also for another seven years of work." ²⁸ So Jacob agreed.*ᶜ*

After Jacob completed the *bridal* week, Laban gave him Rachel as his wife. ²⁹ And he gave his servant Bilhah to Rachel as her maidservant. ³⁰ Jacob slept with Rachel too, and indeed, he loved her more than Leah. Then Jacob worked *for Laban* for seven more years.

Jacob's Sons*ᵈ*

³¹ When the LORD saw that Leah was unloved, he opened her womb; but Rachel was childless. ³² Leah became pregnant and gave birth to a son. She named him Reuben,*ᵉ* saying, "Because the LORD has seen my misery.*ᶠ* Surely my husband will love me now."

³³ She conceived again and gave birth to a son and said, "Because the LORD has heard that I am unloved, he has given me this one also." So she named him Simeon (*i.e.,* One Who Hears).

³⁴ She conceived again, and when she gave birth to a son she said, "Now my husband will become attached to me, because I have borne him three sons." So he was named Levi (*i.e.,* Attached).

³⁵ She conceived again, and when she gave birth to a *fourth* son she said, "This time I will praise the LORD." So she named him Judah (*i.e.,* Praise). Then she stopped bearing children.

Genesis 30

¹ Rachel, seeing that she was not bearing any children for Jacob, became jealous of her sister. So she told Jacob, "Give me children, or I'll die!"

---

a   Literally, "and made a feast."

b   Literally, "it must not be done so in our place."

c   Literally, "did so."

d   Jacob's sons are listed in Genesis 35:23.

e   Perhaps a play on words. "*Reuben*" literally means "see, a son." It sounds like the two-word phrase, "*ruâ beonyi,*" which means "he saw my misery."

f   Or "affliction."

² He became angry and said, "Am I in the place of God? He has kept you from having children."*ᵃ*

³ So she said, "Here is my maidservant, Bilhah. Sleep with her; she can bear children for me, and through her I too can have children." ⁵ And she gave him Bilhah as a wife, so he slept with her, and she conceived and bore him a *fifth* son. ⁶ Then Rachel said, "God has vindicated me. He has listened to my plea and given me a son." So she named him Dan (*i.e.,* He Has Vindicated).

⁷ Then Bilhah conceived and bore Jacob *her* second son, *his sixth.* ⁸ So Rachel said, "I have fought a mighty fight with my sister, and I have won." So she named him Naphtali (*i.e.,* My Struggle).

⁹ When Leah saw that she had stopped having children, she took her servant Zilpah and gave her to Jacob as a wife. ¹⁰ When Zilpah bore Jacob a *seventh* son, ¹¹ Leah exclaimed, "How fortunate!" So she named him Gad (*i.e.,* Good Fortune). ¹² When Zilpah bore Jacob *her* second son (*his eighth*), ¹³ Leah named him Asher (*i.e.,* Happy), saying, "How happy I am. Women will call me happy."

¹⁴ During the wheat harvest, Reuben found some mandrakes*ᵇ* in the field and brought them to his mother Leah. Rachel requested of Leah, "Please give me some of your son's mandrakes."

¹⁵ But she replied, "Isn't it enough that you took my husband? And now you want to take my son's mandrakes too?

So Rachel said. "He may lie with you tonight in return for your son's mandrakes."

¹⁶ So when Jacob came in from the fields that evening, Leah went out to meet him and said, "You must come in to me *tonight,* for I have hired you with my son's mandrakes." So he slept with her that night.

¹⁷ God listened to Leah, and she conceived and bore Jacob *her* fifth son (*his ninth*). ¹⁸ And she said, "God has rewarded me*ᶜ* for giving my maidservant to my husband." So she named him Issachar (*i.e.,* Reward).

¹⁹ Leah conceived again and bore Jacob *her* sixth son (*his tenth*). ²⁰ *This time* she said, "God has presented me with a good gift. Now my husband will honor me, because I have borne him six sons." So she named him Zebulun (*i.e.,* Honor).

²¹ Later she gave birth to a daughter and named her Dinah.

²² Then God remembered Rachel, listened to her, and opened her womb. ²³ She conceived and gave birth to *Jacob's eleventh* son and said, "God has removed my shame. ²⁴ May the LORD add to me another son." So she named him Joseph (*i.e.,* May He Add).

Jacob Becomes Rich

²⁵ After Rachel gave birth to Joseph, Jacob said to Laban, "Send me away so I can go back to my own country. ²⁶ Give me my wives and children for whom I have served you, and let me depart. You know the service I've given you."

²⁷ But Laban said to him, "If it pleases you, *stay.* I have seen the signs;*ᵈ* the LORD has blessed me because of you. ²⁸ Name your wages, and I will pay them."

---

a   Literally, "withheld from you the fruit of the womb."

b   "Mandrake": a poisonous plant that many people believed had special curative and/or evil powers, including the ability to affect sexual desire and procreation.

c   Literally, "given me my wages."

d   Or "learned by divination."

²⁹ Jacob replied, "You know how I served you and how your livestock have fared with me. ³⁰ What little you had before I came increased greatly, and the LORD has blessed you wherever I turned. But when can I do something for my own household?"

³¹ So Laban asked, "What shall I give you?"

Jacob replied, "Don't give me anything. Do this for me and I will keep on pasturing and watching over your flocks. ³² Let me go through your flocks today and remove every speckled, spotted, or black lamb and every speckled or spotted goat. They will be my wages. ³³ And my honesty will speak for itself whenever you come to check my wages. Any goat *found* with me that is not speckled or spotted, or any lamb that is not dark-colored, will be considered stolen."

³⁴ And Laban said, "Agreed; let it be according to your word."

³⁵ That day Jacob removed all the striped or spotted male goats and all the speckled or spotted female goats (every one with white on it) and all the black lambs. He placed them in the care of his sons. ³⁶ Then Jacob put *the space of* a three-day journey between himself and Laban while *his sons* continued pasturing the rest of Laban's flocks.

³⁷ Then Jacob took fresh branches of poplar, almond, and plane trees and *peeled the bark* to make white stripes by exposing the white *inner wood* of the branches. ³⁸ Then he set the rods he had peeled in the gutters and watering troughs*ᵃ* in front of where the flocks came to drink so they would mate when they came to drink.*ᵇ* ³⁹ They mated in front of the branches, and the young they bore were striped or speckled or spotted. ⁴⁰ Jacob separated those lambs and made the rest face Laban's striped and black animals. That way he made separate flocks for himself and kept them from Laban's flock. ⁴¹ Whenever the stronger *females* were in heat, Jacob would place the branches in the troughs*ᶜ* in sight of the flock so they would mate near the branches. ⁴² But if the animals were weak, he would not put them there. So the weaker ones were Laban's and the stronger ones, Jacob's. ⁴³ So he became exceedingly prosperous and had large flocks and male and female servants, camels, and donkeys.

Genesis 31
Jacob Flees Laban

¹ Jacob heard that Laban's sons were complaining, "Jacob has taken all that was our father's and has made all his fortune from it." ² Jacob *also* saw that Laban's attitude toward him was no longer *friendly*.

³ Then the LORD said to him, "Return to the land of your fathers and to your relatives, and I will be with you."

⁴ So Jacob called Rachel and Leah to the field where his flock was. ⁵ He told them, "I see your father's attitude isn't *as friendly* toward me as it was before. But the God of my father has been with me. ⁶ You know that I've served your father with all my strength, ⁷ yet your father has cheated me and changed my wages ten times.

---

a   Or "set the rods he had peeled in the troughs, the watering troughs."

b   Many theories have been proposed for why sheep would mate before peeled branches, all unproven.

c   Or "gutters."

However, God has not allowed him to hurt me. [8] If he said, 'The speckled ones will be your wages,' then the flock produced speckled young; and if he said, 'The streaked ones will be your wages,' then the flock produced streaked young. [9] So God has taken away your father's livestock and given them to me.

[10] "I had a dream in the breeding season.[a] I looked up and saw that the male goats mating with the flock were striped, speckled, and spotted. [11] Then the angel of God in the dream called, 'Jacob.' And I said, 'Here I am.' [12] And he said, 'Look up and see that all the male goats that are mating are streaked, speckled, and spotted, for I have seen all that Laban has been doing to you. [13] I am the God of Bethel, where you anointed the *memorial* pillar and made a vow to me.[b] Now get out of this land at once and return to the land of your birth.'"

[14] Then Rachel and Leah replied, "Do we still have any inheritance of our father's house? [15] Hasn't he treated us as foreigners? He's sold us and used up the money you paid for us. [16] Surely all the wealth that God has taken away from our father belongs to us and our children. So do whatever God has told you."

[17] So Jacob put his children, his wives, and the goods he had accumulated in Paddan Aram on camels [18] and drove them and all his livestock toward his father Isaac in Canaan.

[19] Now Rachel had stolen her father's household gods when Laban had gone to shear his flock. [20] And Jacob, who had deceived Laban the Aramean by not telling him he was fleeing, [21] fled with all he had. He crossed the *Euphrates* River, and headed for[c] the hill country of Gilead.

Jacob and Laban Make Peace

[22] On the third day someone told Laban that Jacob had fled. [23, 25] So Laban took his relatives and pursued him for seven days, and he caught up with him where he had camped in the hill country of Gilead. So Laban and his relatives camped there too. [24] Then God came to Laban in a dream at night and said to him, "Be careful not to say anything to Jacob, either good or bad."

[26] So Laban asked Jacob, "What have you done? You've deceived me and carried off my daughters like captives in war.[d] [27] Why did you flee secretly and deceive me? Why didn't you tell me? I would have sent you away with joy and songs, *with the music of* tambourines and harps. [28] You didn't *even* let me kiss my daughters and grandsons goodbye! What you have done is foolish. [29] I have the power to harm you, but the God of your father spoke to me last night, warning me, 'Be careful to speak nothing either good or bad to Jacob.' [30] Now *I understand that* you went because you longed to return to your father's house. But why did you steal my gods?"

[31] Jacob replied, "I was afraid. I thought that perhaps you would take your daughters by force. [32] But the one with whom you find your gods shall not live. In the presence of our relatives, point out what is yours and take it." For Jacob did not know that Rachel had stolen the gods.

---

a Literally, "when the flocks were mating."
b See Genesis 28:18.
c Literally, "set his face toward."
d Literally, "captives of the sword."

48

³³ So Laban went into Jacob's tent and Leah's tent and the tent of the two maidservants, but he didn't find them. Then he left Leah's tent and entered Rachel's tent. ³⁴ Now Rachel had taken the household gods and put them in her camel's saddle and was sitting on them. Laban searched the whole tent but found nothing.

³⁵ Rachel said to him, "My lord, don't be angry that I cannot stand for you, for my time of the month*a* is upon me." So he searched but couldn't find the household gods.

³⁶ Then Jacob got angry and challenged Laban. "What's my offense?" he demanded. "What's my sin that you should chase after me so fervently? ³⁷ Now that you've searched through all my goods, what of your household goods have you found? Put it here in front of our relatives, and let them judge between us. ³⁸ I've been with you for twenty years. Your sheep and goats have not miscarried, and I have not eaten your rams. ³⁹ I did not bring you *animals* torn *by wild beasts;* I bore the loss myself. And you sought payment from me*b* for whatever was stolen in daylight or nighttime. ⁴⁰ There I was: consumed by heat in the daytime and cold at night. Sleep fled from my eyes. ⁴¹ For twenty years I was in your house. I worked fourteen years for your two daughters, and for six years *I watched* your flocks—*yet* you changed my wages ten times. ⁴² If the God of my father, the God of Abraham, and your fear of Isaac had not been with me, surely you would have sent me away empty-handed. But God has seen my affliction and the labor of my hands, and last night he rebuked you, *not me."c*

⁴³ Laban replied, "These daughters are my daughters; these children are my children. The flocks are my flocks. All you see is mine. But what can I do today for these my daughters or for the children they have borne? ⁴⁴ Come now, let's make a covenant, you and I, and let it serve as evidence*d* between us *that we made peace."*

⁴⁵ So Jacob took a stone and set it up as a *memorial* pillar. ⁴⁶ Then he said to his relatives, "Gather stones." And they took stones and piled them in a heap, and they ate *a covenant meal* by it. Jacob called it Galeed (*Hebrew meaning* Witness Heap)

⁴⁷ Laban called it Jegar Sahadutha (*Aramaic meaning* Witness Heap), ⁴⁸ and saying, "Today this heap stands as a witness*e* between you and me." That is why it was named Galeed. ⁴⁹ It was also called Mizpah (*i.e.,* Watchtower) because he said, "May the LORD watch between you and me when we are away from each other. ⁵⁰ If you mistreat my daughters or if you take any wives besides my daughters, even though no one is with us, remember that God is a witness *to this covenant* between you and me. ⁵¹ See this heap and this pillar I have set up between you and me. ⁵² This heap is a witness and this pillar is a witness that I will not go past this heap to your side to harm you, and that you will not go past this heap and pillar to harm me. ⁵³ May the God of Abraham and the God of Nahor,*f* the God of their father *Terah,* judge between us."

So Jacob swore by the fear of his father Isaac. ⁵⁴ He offered a sacrifice in the hill country and called his relatives to the *covenant* meal. After they had eaten, they spent the night on the mountain. ⁵⁵ And early in the morning Laban kissed his daughters and grandchildren and blessed them. Then he returned home.

---

a Literally, "the manner of women."

b Literally, "required it from my hand."

c Or "last night he rendered judgement."

d Literally, "as a witness."

e Literally, "this heap is a witness."

f Nahor and Terah were polytheistic (see Joshua 24:2, 15). It seems here that Yahweh was one of their gods.

Genesis 32
Jacob Prepares to Meet Esau

¹ As Jacob went on his way, the angels of God met him. ² When he saw them, he said, "This is the camp of God!" So he named that place Mahanaim (i.e., two camps).[a]

³ Jacob sent messengers to his brother Esau in Seir in Edom. ⁴ He instructed them, "Tell this to my lord Esau: 'Your servant Jacob says, "I have lived temporarily with Laban until now. ⁵ I have cattle and donkeys, flocks, menservants and maidservants. I have sent *messengers* to tell my lord, that I might find favor in your sight."'"

⁶ The messengers returned to Jacob and warned him, "We went to Esau, and he's coming to meet you—with four hundred men!"

⁷ Terrified,[b] Jacob divided the flocks and herds and camels and the people who were with him into two camps. ⁸ He thought, "If Esau attacks one group, the other[c] group may escape."

⁹ Then he prayed, "O God of my father Abraham, God of my father Isaac, O LORD who said to me, 'Return to your country and to your relatives, and I will deal well with you,[d] ¹⁰ I am unworthy of all the lovingkindness that you have faithfully shown[e] your servant; for I crossed the Jordan with *only* my staff, and now I have become two camps. ¹¹ Deliver me, I pray, from the hand of my brother, from the hand of Esau. I'm afraid he'll come and attack me and the mothers and children. ¹² You promised, 'I will surely deal well with you and make your descendants like the sands of the sea—too great to be counted.'"

¹³ Then he spent the night there and selected a gift for Esau from what he had at hand:

- ¹⁴ Two hundred female goats
- Twenty male goats
- Two hundred ewes
- Twenty rams
- ¹⁵ Thirty milking camels with their calves
- Forty other cows
- Ten bulls
- Twenty female donkeys
- Ten male donkeys

¹⁶ He put them in the care of[f] his servants, each herd by itself, and told them "Go ahead *of us,* and keep some space between the herds." ¹⁷ He instructed the first, "When Esau asks, 'Who do you belong to? Where are you going? Who owns all these animals?' ¹⁸ tell him, 'They belong to your servant Jacob. They are a gift sent to my lord Esau. He is coming behind us.'" ¹⁹ He also told everyone who followed the herds,[g] "Say the same thing when you meet Esau. ²⁰ Be sure to say, 'Your servant Jacob is coming behind us.'" (He was thinking, "I will pacify him *by sending* gifts ahead of me. Later, when I see him face *to face,* perhaps he will accept me.") ²¹ So the gifts went on ahead of him, but he spent the night in the camp.

---

a   "Two camps": perhaps referring to his camp and God's camp.
b   Literally, "Jacob was greatly afraid and distressed."
c   Literally, "remaining."
d   See Genesis 31:3.
e   Or "all the lovingkindness and faithfulness that you have shown."
f   Literally, "delivered them into the hand of."
g   Literally, "the second and third and all who followed the herds."

Jacob Wrestles and Is Named "Israel"

[22] That night Jacob got up, took his two wives, his two maidservants, and his eleven sons, and crossed the ford of the Jabbok. [23] *First* he took them and sent them across the stream. Then he sent over everything else. [24] So Jacob was left alone, and a man[a] wrestled with him till daybreak.

[25] When the man saw that he couldn't prevail, as they wrestled he touched Jacob's hip socket so that it became dislocated, [26] and he said, "Let me go—it's daybreak!"

But Jacob replied, "I won't let you go unless you bless me."

[27] The man asked, "What is your name?"

He replied, "Jacob."

[28] "Your name will no longer be Jacob," the man declared, "but *you will be called* Israel (*i.e.,* He Struggles with God; *or* God Prevails) because you have wrestled with God and with men and have overcome."[b]

[29] Then Jacob asked him, "Please tell me your name."

And he replied, "Why do you ask me my name?" And there he blessed him.

[30] So Jacob called the place Peniel (*i.e.,* Face of God), saying, "I have seen God face to face, and yet my life has been spared." [31] The sun rose upon him as he left Penuel,[c] limping because of his hip. [32] Thus, to this day, Israelites do not eat the tendon *attached to* the socket of the hip, because he touched the socket of Jacob's hip near the tendon.

Genesis 33
Jacob Meets Esau

[1] Jacob looked up and saw Esau coming with his four hundred men. So he divided the children among Leah and Rachel and their two maidservants, *Bilhah and Zilpah.* [2] Then he put the maidservants and their children in front, Leah and her children next, and Rachel and Joseph last. [3] He went on ahead and bowed down to the ground seven times[d] as he approached his brother. [4] But Esau ran to meet him, embraced him, threw his arms around his neck, and kissed him; and they wept. [5] Then Esau looked up and saw the women and children. "Who are these *people?*" he asked.

Jacob answered, "The children God has graciously given to your servant."

[6] Then the maidservants approached with their children and bowed down. [7] Then Leah and her children came and bowed down. And afterward, Joseph and Rachel came and bowed down. [8] So Esau asked, "What do you mean by all these servants and animals[e] I have come upon?"

Jacob replied, "*A gift*, to find favor in your sight, my lord."

[9] But Esau said, "I have plenty, my brother. Keep what you have for yourself."

[10] But Jacob insisted, "No, please! If I have found favor in your sight, take this present from my hand. Seeing your face is like seeing the face of God—and you have accepted me! [11] Please accept my gift,[f] for God has been gracious to me and I have all *I need.*" And because Jacob insisted, Esau accepted.

[12] Then Esau said, "Let's head out. I'll lead."

---

a   Hosea 12:4 tells us that the man was an angel.

b   Throughout the rest of the Bible Jacob is referred to sometimes as Jacob and sometimes as Israel.

c   The reason the place name is spelled differently than in the previous sentence is not clear.

d   Bowing seven times was a common ceremonial act of dignitaries.

e   Literally, "all this camp."

f   Literally, "my gift which has been brought to you."

[13] But Jacob replied, "My lord knows that the children are frail and that I must care for the nursing ewes and cows and their young. If they are driven hard even one day, all the flocks will die. [14] So please, my lord, go on ahead of your servant. I'll move along slowly at the pace of the herds and the children until I come to my lord in Seir."

[15] Esau said, "Please let me leave some of my men with you."

But Jacob objected, "Why do that? Just let me find favor in the sight of my lord."

So that day Esau returned *south to* the Seir Highlands. [17] But Jacob went *west* to Succoth, where he built himself a house and made shelters for his livestock. That's why the place is called Succoth (*i.e.,* Shelter).

[18] After Jacob returned from Paddan Aram, he arrived safely at Shechem in Canaan and he camped near the city. [19] He bought the land where he pitched his tent from the sons of Hamor (the father of Shechem) for a hundred pieces of money.[a] [20] Then he erected an altar there and called it El Elohe Israel (*i.e.,* God, the God of Israel; *or* Mighty is the God of Israel).

Genesis 34
Shechem Rapes Dinah

[1] Now Dinah, Jacob's daughter by Leah,[b] went out to visit the women of the land. [2] Shechem (the son of the region's ruler, Hamor the Hivite) saw her, took her, and raped her. [3] And he was captivated by her and fell in love with her, so he spoke tenderly to her. [4] And he told his father Hamor, "Get me this girl for my wife."

[5] Jacob's sons were in the fields *tending* livestock when he heard that Shechem had raped Dinah, so he kept quiet about it until they came home. [6] Shechem's father Hamor went to speak to Jacob, [7] and Jacob's sons came in from the fields as soon as they heard. They were grieved and very angry because Shechem had done such a disgraceful thing by lying with Jacob's daughter, a thing that ought not to be done in Israel.

[8] So Hamor spoke to them: "My son's soul longs for your daughter. Please give her to him as his wife. [9] Intermarry with us. Give us your daughters and take our daughters. [10] Settle among us; the land is open to you. Live in it, trade, and get property there."

[11] And Shechem begged her father and brothers, "Let me find favor in your sight, and I will give you whatever you ask. [12] Ask for a marriage price and gift as great as you like, and I'll pay it. Just give me the girl as my wife."

Simeon and Levi Take Revenge

[13] Jacob's sons replied deceitfully to Shechem and his father, Hamor, because Dinah had been raped: [14] "We cannot do this. We cannot give our sister to a man who's uncircumcised. To us that would be a disgrace. [15] We'll give consent to you only on this *condition*: You become like us—all your men must be circumcised. [16] Then we will give you our daughters and take your daughters. We'll live with you and become one people. [17] But if you do not listen, *agree* to be circumcised, we'll take our sister and go."

[18] Their words seemed good to Hamor and Shechem. [19] The young man (the most honored *person* of all in his father's household) did not delay doing what they said because he desired Jacob's daughter. [20] Then Hamor and Shechem went to the city gate and spoke to the men. He told them, [21] "These men are friendly toward us.

---

a Literally, "one hundred kesitahs." The value or weight of a kesitah is unknown.
b Literally, "the daughter of Leah whom she had borne to Jacob."

Let them live in our land and trade in it. Look, the land is large enough for them. We can take their daughters and give them ours *in marriage.* 22 But they will consent to live with us as one people only on the condition that every male among us be circumcised, *just* as they are. 23 Won't all their livestock, their *other* animals, and their property become ours? So let's give our consent, and they will live among us."

24 And all who went through the city gate listened to Hamor and Shechem, and every male in the city*a* was circumcised.

25 Three days later, while they were still in pain, two of Jacob's sons, Dinah's brothers Simeon and Levi, took their swords and attacked the *so-called* "secure city" without warning. They killed every man. 26 *After* they had slain Hamor and his son Shechem with the edge of their sword, they took Dinah from Shechem's house and left. 27 Jacob's *other* sons came upon the dead and looted the city because their sister had been defiled. 28 They took their flocks, herds, donkeys, and everything else in the city and the fields. 29 They plundered all their wealth, everything in the houses, and took captive all their women and children.

30 Then Jacob told Simeon and Levi, "You've brought trouble on me by making me odious to the inhabitants of this land, the Canaanites and Perizzites. They will join forces against me and attack. We are few in number, so I and my household will be wiped out."

31 But they replied, "Should he have treated our sister like a whore?"

Genesis 35
Jacob Returns to Bethel

1 Then God said to Jacob, "Go up to Bethel and settle there. Build an altar there to *me,* the God who appeared to you when you fled from your brother Esau."

2 So Jacob said to his household and to everyone with him, "Get rid of the foreign gods you have with you. Purify*b* yourselves and change your clothes. 3 Then we must go to Bethel, so I may build an altar to God, who answered me in the day of my distress and who has been with me wherever I have gone." 4 So they gave Jacob all their foreign gods and earrings, and he hid them under the oak near Shechem. 5 As they journeyed, the terror of God was on the towns around them so that no one pursued them.

6 When Jacob and his people came to Luz in Canaan (that is, Bethel, *which means* House of God), 7 he built an altar. He called the spot El Bethel (*i.e.,* God of Bethel) because there God had revealed himself to him when he fled from his brother.

8 Then Deborah, Rebekah's nurse, died. She was buried below Bethel under the oak. So it was named Allon Bacuth (*i.e.,* Oak of Weeping).

Jacob Reaffirmed as "Israel"

9 God appeared to Jacob again (*as he did* when Jacob had come from Paddan Aram*c*). 10 He blessed him, saying "Your name is Jacob (*i.e.,* "He Grasps the Heel"*d*) but you will no longer be called Jacob. Your name will be Israel*e* (*i.e.,* He Struggles with

---

a Literally, "every male who went out of the gate of the city." The meaning of the term is not clear.

b Hebrew: *taher.* It can refer to having a disease, or to being clean physically or ceremonially.

c See Genesis 32:22–32.

d Or figuratively, "He Deceives."

e Throughout the rest of the Bible, Jacob is referred to sometimes as Jacob and sometimes as Israel.

God[a]." So he called him "Israel." [11] And God continued, "I am El Shaddai (i.e., God Almighty). Be fruitful and multiply. A nation and a company of nations will come from you. Kings will come from your body.[b] [12] The land which I gave to Abraham and Isaac I also will give to you, and I will give it to your descendants after you." [13] Then God went up from him, from the place where he had spoken to him.

[14] Jacob set up a *memorial* pillar at the place where God had talked with him, a pillar of stone. He poured a drink offering on it and poured oil on it.[c] [15] He called the place where God had talked to him Bethel.[d] [16] Then they left Bethel.

Rachel Dies

While they were still a ways from Ephrath, Rachel began to give birth and had hard labor. [17] While she was in heavy labor the midwife said, "Don't be afraid, for now you have another son."

[18] As her soul was departing (for she was dying), she named him Ben-Oni (i.e., Son of My Sorrow). But Jacob called him Benjamin (i.e., Son of My Right Hand). [19] So Rachel died and was buried on the way to Ephrath (that is, Bethlehem). [20] Jacob set up a pillar over her grave which marks it to this day.

---

a Or "God Prevails."
b Literally, "from your loins."
c "Poured oil on it:" An act of anointing, signifying something as now set apart for god's service..
d See Genesis 28:19.

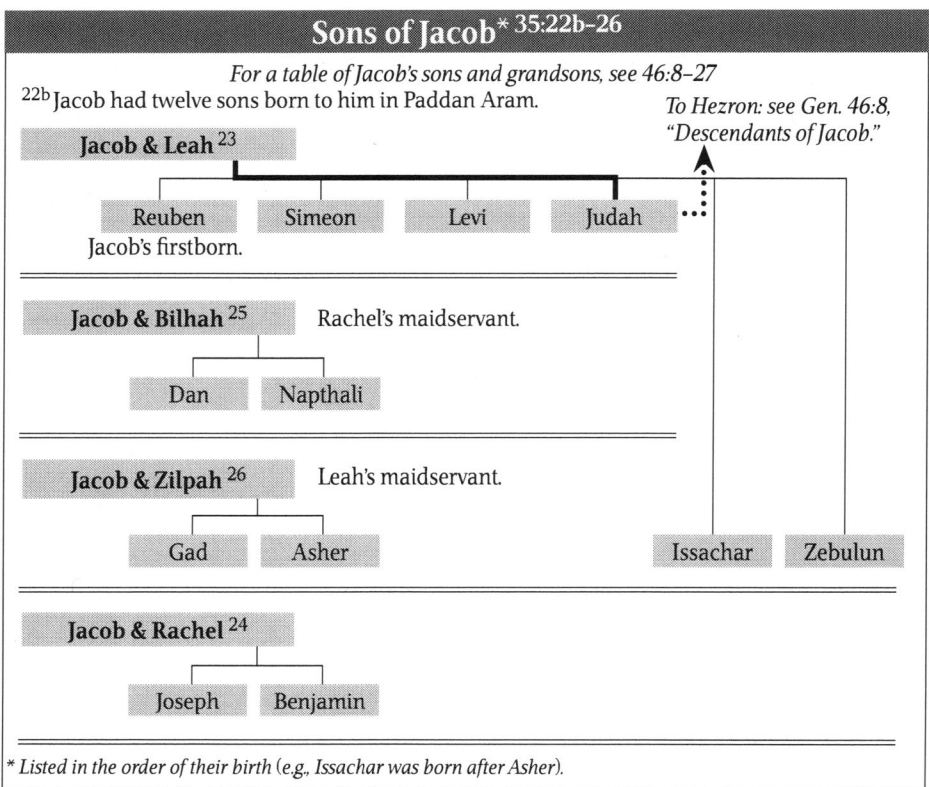

Sons of Jacob* 35:22b-26

For a table of Jacob's sons and grandsons, see 46:8–27

[22b] Jacob had twelve sons born to him in Paddan Aram.

To Hezron: see Gen. 46:8, "Descendants of Jacob."

Jacob & Leah [23]

Reuben — Jacob's firstborn.
Simeon
Levi
Judah

Jacob & Bilhah [25]   Rachel's maidservant.

Dan
Napthali

Jacob & Zilpah [26]   Leah's maidservant.

Gad
Asher
Issachar
Zebulun

Jacob & Rachel [24]

Joseph
Benjamin

* Listed in the order of their birth (e.g., Issachar was born after Asher).

²¹ Israel moved on and pitched his tent beyond Migdal Eder (*i.e.,* Tower of Eder). ^{22a} While he was living in that land, Reuben slept with Bilhah, his father's concubine, and Israel heard of it.

Isaac Dies

²⁷ Jacob came home to his father Isaac in Mamre, near Kiriath Arba (*i.e.,* Hebron), where Abraham and Isaac had lived as foreigners. ²⁸ Isaac lived *to be* one hundred and eighty years old. ²⁹ Then he breathed his last and died and was gathered to his people at a ripe old age. And his sons Esau and Jacob buried him.

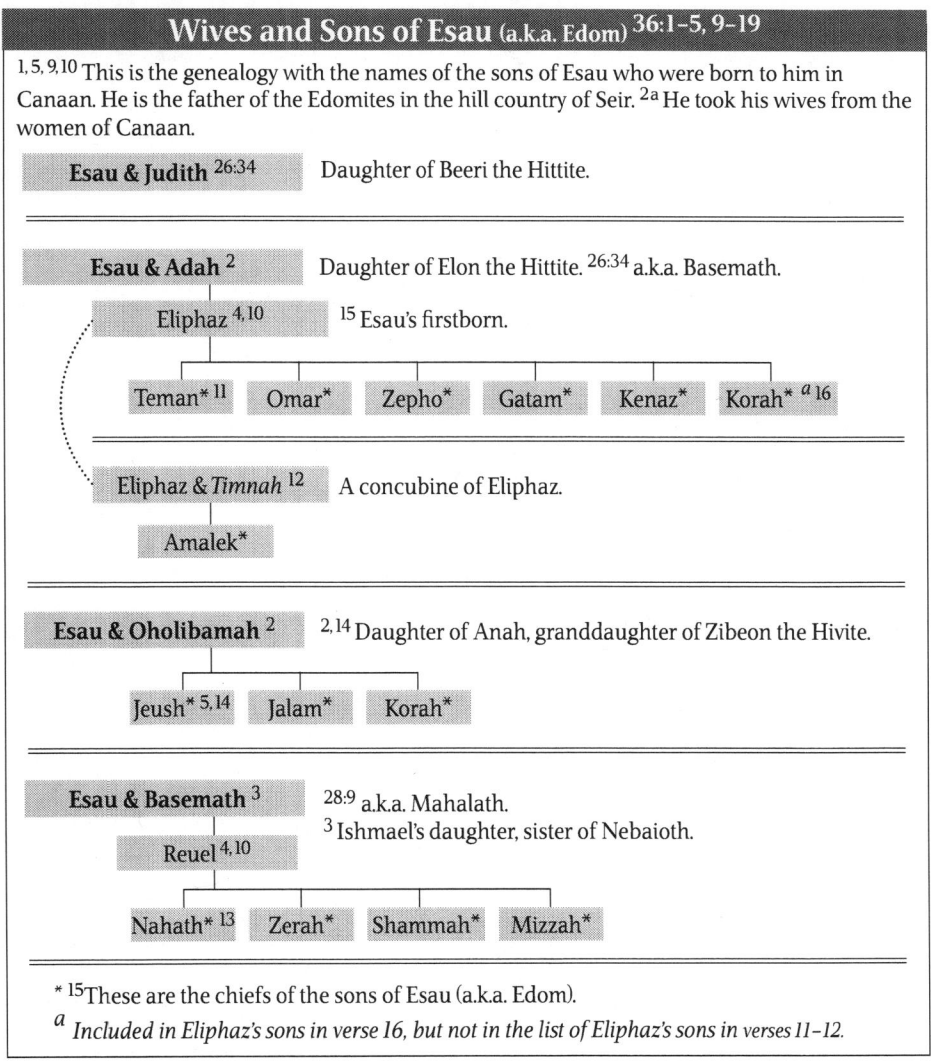

Wives and Sons of Esau (a.k.a. Edom) 36:1–5, 9–19

^{1, 5, 9,10} This is the genealogy with the names of the sons of Esau who were born to him in Canaan. He is the father of the Edomites in the hill country of Seir. ^{2a} He took his wives from the women of Canaan.

Esau & Judith ^{26:34}   Daughter of Beeri the Hittite.

Esau & Adah ²   Daughter of Elon the Hittite. ^{26:34} a.k.a. Basemath.

Eliphaz ^{4, 10}   ¹⁵ Esau's firstborn.

Teman*¹¹ Omar* Zepho* Gatam* Kenaz* Korah* ^{a 16}

Eliphaz & *Timnah* ¹²   A concubine of Eliphaz.

Amalek*

Esau & Oholibamah ²   ^{2, 14} Daughter of Anah, granddaughter of Zibeon the Hivite.

Jeush*^{5, 14} Jalam* Korah*

Esau & Basemath ³   ^{28:9} a.k.a. Mahalath.
³ Ishmael's daughter, sister of Nebaioth.

Reuel ^{4, 10}

Nahath*¹³ Zerah* Shammah* Mizzah*

* ¹⁵These are the chiefs of the sons of Esau (a.k.a. Edom).

^a *Included in Eliphaz's sons in verse 16, but not in the list of Eliphaz's sons in verses 11–12.*

Jacob and Esau Separate

⁷ The land where Jacob and his brother Esau lived at the moment could not support them *both* because of their livestock. *That is,* their possessions were too numerous for them to remain *close* together. ⁶ So Esau took his wives, his sons, his daughters, and all the members of his household, his livestock, all his beasts, and all his property that he had acquired in the land of Canaan, and moved into a land away from his brother Jacob. ⁸ Thus Esau (that is, Edom) settled in the Seir Highlands.

Verses 9–19 are above in "Wives and Sons of Esau."

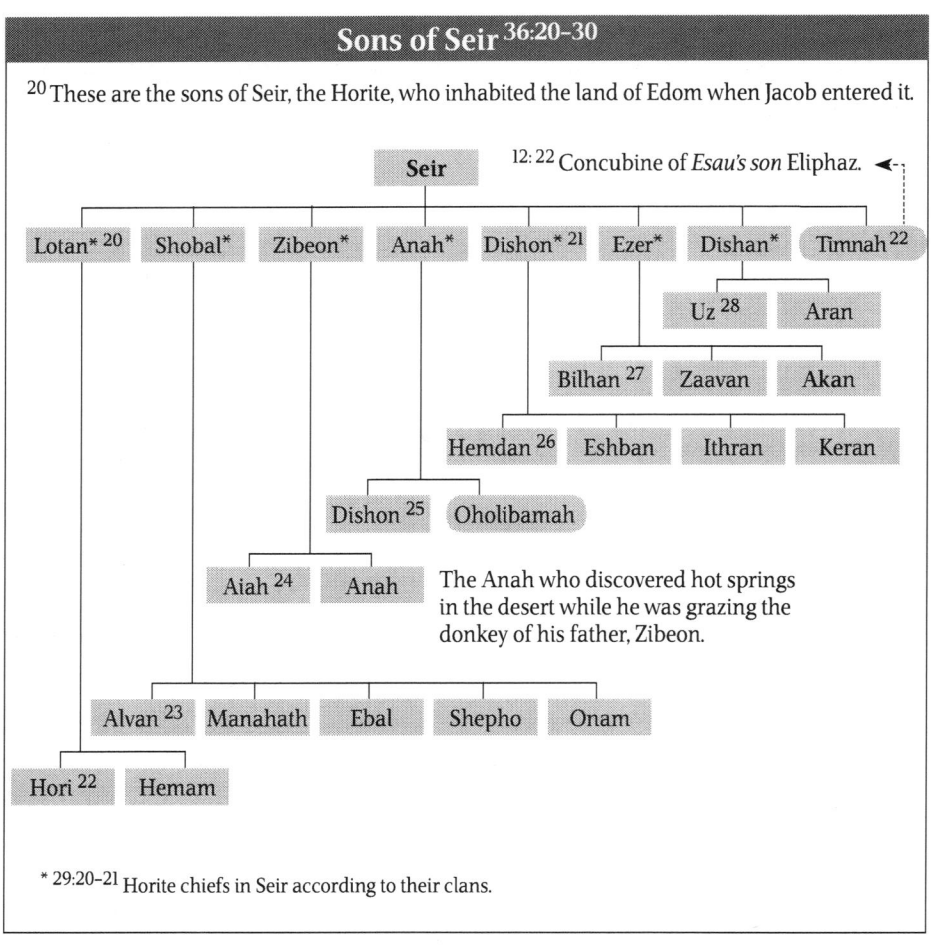

Sons of Seir 36:20-30

²⁰ These are the sons of Seir, the Horite, who inhabited the land of Edom when Jacob entered it.

12: 22 Concubine of *Esau's son* Eliphaz.

The Anah who discovered hot springs in the desert while he was grazing the donkey of his father, Zibeon.

* 29:20-21 Horite chiefs in Seir according to their clans.

Kings of Edom 36:31-39

³¹ These are the kings of Edom who reigned before any king reigned over the Israelites.

King	City	
Bela ³²	Dinhabah	Son of Beor.
Jobab* ³³		Son of Zerah of Bozrah.
Husham* ³⁴		Of the land of the Temanites.
Hadad* ³⁵	Avith	Son of Bedad (who defeated Midian in the field of Moab).
Samlah* ³⁶		From Masrekah.
Shaul* ³⁷		From Rehoboth on the *Euphrates* River.**
Baal-Hanan* ³⁸		Son of Acbor.
Hadad* ³⁹	Pau	His wife was Mehetabel, the daughter of Matred and granddaughter of Me-Zahab.

* *These* became king when the preceding king died.
** Or "from Rehoboth-on-the-River."

Chiefs of Edom

⁴⁰, ⁴³ These are the chiefs who descended from Esau*a* (father of the Edomites) according to their families, regions, and settlements:

- Timna ⁴⁰
- Alvah
- Jetheth

- Oholibamah ⁴¹
- Elah
- Pinon

- Kenaz ⁴²
- Teman
- Mibzar

- Magdiel ⁴³
- Iram

Genesis 37
Joseph's Dreams

¹ This is *a continuation of the family history* of the descendants of Jacob, *who* lived in Canaan where his father had dwelled.

² When Joseph was seventeen years old, he tended the flocks with his brothers. He was *but* a youth, *working with* the sons of his father's wives Zilpah and Bilhah, *his half-brothers.* One day he brought their father a bad report about them. ³

³ Now Israel loved Joseph more than any of his *other* sons because he was the son of his old age. Thus he made him a multicolored robe.*b* ⁴ When his brothers saw that their father loved him more than any of them, they hated him and could not speak to him peacefully.

⁵ When Joseph had a dream and told it to them, they hated him even more. ⁶ "Listen to this dream I had," he said. ⁷ "We were tying up bundles of grain in the field when suddenly my bundle rose and stood erect. Your bundles gathered around mine and bowed down!"

⁸ His brothers replied, "Do you actually *expect* to reign over us? To rule us?" So they hated him even more because of his dream and what he had said.

---

a Literally, "chiefs of Esau."
b Or "ornate robe."

⁹ Then he had another dream, and he told it to his brothers. "Listen, I had another dream. The sun and moon and eleven stars were bowing down to me!"

¹⁰ When he recounted it to his father and brothers, Israel rebuked him. "What is this dream you dreamed? Will your mother and I and your brothers actually come and bow down to the ground before you?" ¹¹ And his brothers were jealous of him, but his father kept the words in mind.ᵃ

Joseph Sold into Slavery

¹² When Joseph's brothers went to graze their father's flock near Shechem, ¹³ ¹³ Israel told him, "Aren't your brothers grazing the flock near Shechem? Come, I am going to send you to them."

"I will go," he replied.

¹⁴ Israel said, "Go and see if all is well with your brothers and the flock, and bring word back to me." And he sent him from the Valley of Hebron to Shechem.

¹⁵ A man found him wandering the fields and asked, "Who are you looking for?"

¹⁶ "I'm looking for my brothers," he replied. "Please tell me where they are grazing *their flocks.*"

¹⁷ The man said, "They have moved from here. I heard them say, 'Let's go to Dothan.'" So Joseph went after his brothers and found them near Dothan.

¹⁸ When they saw him in the distance,ᵇ they plotted to kill him, ¹⁹ saying to each other, "Here comes the dreamer! ²⁰ Come on, let's kill him and throw him into one of the cisterns. We'll say that a wild beast devoured him. Then we'll see what comes of his dreams."

²¹ When Reuben heard this, he tried to save him,ᶜ pleading, "We must not take his life. ²² Don't shed any blood. Throw him into this cistern here in the wilderness, but don't lay a hand on him." Reuben said this hoping to rescue him and return him to his father.

²³ So when Joseph came to his brothers, they stripped him of the robe that he wore, the many-colored one.ᵈ ²⁴ And they took him and threw him into a cistern—an empty one with no water in it.

²⁵ Then they sat down to eat a meal, and they looked upᵉ and saw a caravan of Ishmaelites coming from Gilead on their way to Egypt. Their camels bore spices,ᶠ balm, and myrrh.ᵍ ²⁶ Judah said to his brothers, "What will we gain if we kill our brother and cover up his blood? ²⁷ Come, let's sell him to the Ishmaelites and not lay our hands on him; for he is our brother, our own flesh." His brothers agreed.

²⁸ So when some Midianiteʰ traders passed by, they pulled Joseph up out of the cistern and sold him to the Ishmaelites for seven ounces of silver.ⁱ And the traders took him to Egypt.

---

a   Literally, "observed the saying." That is, "observed what was spoken."
b   Literally, "in the distance, before he came near them."
c   Literally, "rescue him out of their hands."
d   See second footnote in Genesis 37, "Robe of many colors."
e   Literally, "raised their eyes."
f   Or "aromatic gum."
g   "Myrrh": an aromatic tree resin.
h   "Midianite": an Ishmaelite people group who lived primarily on the eastern side of the Gulf of Aqaba.
i   Literally, "twenty *pieces* of silver."

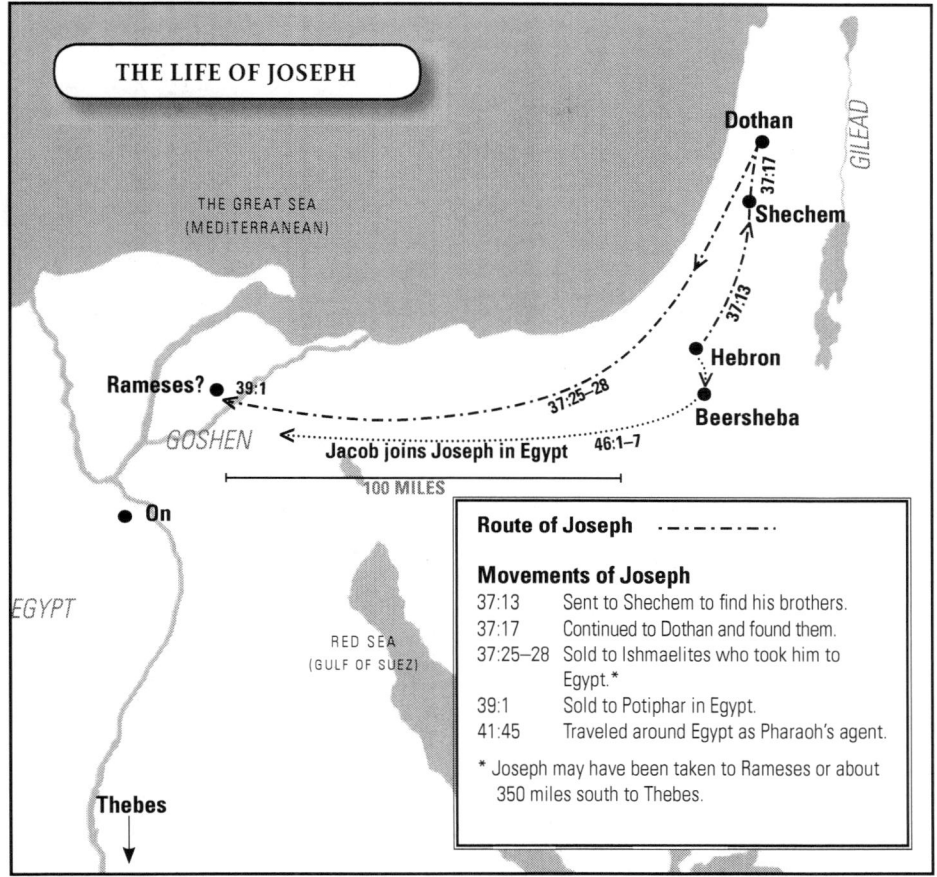

THE LIFE OF JOSEPH

Dothan

GILEAD

37:17

Shechem

THE GREAT SEA
(MEDITERRANEAN)

37:13

Hebron

Rameses? ● 39:1

37:25-28

Beersheba

GOSHEN ← Jacob joins Joseph in Egypt 46:1-7

100 MILES

● On

Route of Joseph · — · — · — · ·

Movements of Joseph

37:13	Sent to Shechem to find his brothers.
37:17	Continued to Dothan and found them.
37:25–28	Sold to Ishmaelites who took him to Egypt.*
39:1	Sold to Potiphar in Egypt.
41:45	Traveled around Egypt as Pharaoh's agent.

* Joseph may have been taken to Rameses or about 350 miles south to Thebes.

EGYPT

RED SEA
(GULF OF SUEZ)

Thebes

29 When Reuben returned to the cistern and *saw that* Joseph was not in it, he tore his clothes.[a] 30 He returned to his brothers and said, "The boy isn't there! Where can I go now?"[b]

31 Then they slaughtered a goat and took Joseph's many-colored robe[c] and dipped it in the blood. 32 They took it back to their father and said, "We found this. Please examine it to see if it is your son's robe."

33 He recognized it and said, "It is my son's robe! Some wild beast has eaten him. Joseph has surely been torn to pieces!" 34 Then Jacob tore his clothes, put on sackcloth,[d] and mourned for his son many days. 35 All his sons and daughters rose to comfort him, but he refused to be comforted, moaning, "In mourning will I go down to Sheol to my son." So his father wept for him.

36 Meanwhile, in Egypt the Midianites sold Joseph to Potiphar, Pharaoh's officer, captain of the guard.

---

a   "Tore his clothes": a customary act to create an outward sign of internal anguish.

b   Literally, "and I, where shall I go."

c   See footnote on "robe of many colors" in paragraph three of this chapter.

d   Literally, "put sackcloth on his loins." "Sackcloth": very rough fabric, worn as sign of mourning.

Genesis 38
Judah's Sons

¹ At that time, Judah left his brothers and went down to stay with Hirah, an Adullamite. ² There Judah met and married*a* the daughter of Shua, a Canaanite. ³ He slept with her, and she conceived and gave birth to a son—and he named him Er. ⁴ She conceived again and gave birth to a son she named Onan. ⁵ She gave birth to still another son and named him Shelah. It was at Kezib that she bore him.*b*

Judah and Tamar

⁶ Judah took a wife for his firstborn, Er, and her name was Tamar. ⁷ But Er was wicked in the Lord's sight, so the Lord killed him.

⁷ Then Judah told Onan, "Lie with your brother's wife and perform your duty*c* to raise offspring for your brother." ⁹ But Onan knew that the descendants would not be *considered as* his, so whenever he went to his brother's wife, he wasted *his semen* on the ground to keep from providing descendants to his brother. ¹⁰ This was wicked in the Lord's sight, so he killed him also.

¹¹ So Judah told his daughter-in-law, Tamar, "Remain a widow in your father's house until my son Shelah grows up." For he thought, "He may also die like his brothers." So Tamar went to live in her father's house.

¹² After a long time Judah's wife (Shua's daughter) died. When the time of mourning was ended, he and his friend Hirah the Adullamite went to Timnah *to see* his sheepshearers.

¹³ When someone said to Tamar, "Look, your father-in-law is going to Timnah to shear his sheep," ¹⁴ she took off her widow's clothes, covered herself with a veil, and disguised*d* herself, and she sat on the road to Timnah at the entrance to Enaim. For she knew*e* that Shelah had grown up, and she had not been given to him as his wife.

¹⁵-¹⁶ When Judah saw her he did not recognize her as his daughter-in-law because she had covered her face. He thought she was a prostitute. So he went to her and said, "Please, let me come in to you."

And she said, "And what will you give me to come in to me?"

¹⁷ He replied, "I'll send you a young goat from the flock."

She responded, "Will you give me a pledge until you send *it*?"

¹⁸ He asked, "What pledge should I give?"

She said, "Your signet ring, your cord, and the staff in your hand."

So he gave them to her and went in to her, and she became pregnant. ¹⁹ She arose and left, took off her veil, and put on her widow's clothes.

²⁰ Judah sent his Adullamite friend with a young goat to get back*f* his pledge from the woman's hand, but he didn't find her. ²¹ He asked the men of the place, "Where is the sacred prostitute*g* who was by the road at Enaim?"

---

a Literally, "took."
b Or "He was in Kezib when she bore him."
c Hebrew: *yibbum*, the duty to marry a dead brother's childless wife and have children to be his heirs.
d Literally, "wrapped."
e Literally, "saw."
f Literally, "receive."
g "Sacred prostitute": a prostitute who practices prostitution as fertility god worship.

They said, "There hasn't been any sacred prostitute here."

²² So he went back to Judah and said, "I didn't find her. And the men of the place said, 'There hasn't been any sacred prostitute here.'"

²³ So Judah said, "Let her keep *what she has*, or we will become the object of ridicule. After all, I sent this young goat, but you didn't find her."

²⁴ About three months later Judah was told, "Your daughter-in-law Tamar has played the harlot and is pregnant by her immorality."

Judah said, "Bring her out and let her be burned *to death*."

²⁵ But as she was being brought out, she sent *the following* message to her father-in-law: "I am pregnant by the man who owns these. Now, whose signet ring and cord and staff are these?"

²⁶ Judah recognized them and said, "She is more righteous than I, since I didn't give her to my son Shelah." And he did not lie with her again.

²⁷ When the time to give birth came, there were twins in her womb. ²⁸ When she was in labor, one put out his hand. So the midwife tied a scarlet thread on his hand and said, "This one came out first." ²⁹ But then he drew back his hand, and his brother came out! She said, "You have broken out!" And he was named Perez (*i.e.,* Break Out). ³⁰ Then his brother, who had the scarlet thread on his hand, came out. And they named him Zerah (*i.e.,* Scarlet; *or* Brightness).

Genesis 39
Joseph and Potiphar's Wife

¹ Now Joseph had been taken to Egypt. Potiphar, an Egyptian who was Pharaoh's captain of the guard, bought him from the Ishmaelites.ᵃ ² The LORD was with Joseph, so he prospered; and he lived in the house of his Egyptian master. ³ His master saw that the LORD was with him and how the LORD gave him success in everything.ᵇ ⁴ So Joseph found favor in Potiphar's sight, and he became his personal servant. Potiphar put him in charge of his household and all that he owned. ⁵ Thenᶜ the LORD blessed the Egyptian's household, all that he had in the house and in the field, because of Joseph. ⁶ So Potiphar left everything in Joseph's charge and did not concern himself with anything except the food he ate.

Now Joseph was well built and handsome. ⁷ Eventually his master's wife looked with desire at Joseph and said, "Lie with me."

⁸ But he refused, saying, "My master does not concern himself with anything in the house with me in charge. He has put everything he owns in my care. ⁹ No one in this house is greater than I am. He has withheld nothing from me except you, because you are his wife. How then could I do such an evil thing and sin against God?" ¹⁰ Day after day she spoke to Joseph, but he would not sleep with her or even be with her.

¹¹ One day he went into the house to do his work and none of the household servants were inside. ¹² She grabbed him by his garment and said, "Lie with me!" But he ran outside, leaving his cloak in her hand. ¹³ When she saw that he had left

---

a   Literally, "the Ishmaelites who had brought him there."

b   Literally, "in whatever he was doing, God caused it to prosper in his hand."

c   Literally, "from the time he put him over his house and all he owned."

his cloak in her hand and had run outside, ¹⁴ she called the men of the house and said, "Look, my husband brought this Hebrew to us to humiliate us!ᵃ He came in to lie with me, but I screamed. ¹⁵ When he heard me call out *for help,* he left his cloak beside me and ran outside."

¹⁶ She kept his cloak beside her until Potiphar came home. ¹⁷ Then she told him, "That Hebrew slave you brought us came to me to make a fool out of me. ¹⁸ When I screamed, he left his cloak beside me and ran out."

¹⁹ When he heard her storyᵇ (*especially* when she said, "This is how your slave treated me"), he burned with anger. ²⁰ He took Joseph and put him in prison, the place where the king's prisoners were confined.

But while Joseph was in jail, ²¹ the LORD was with him. He treated him kindly and gave him favor in the sight of the chief jailer. ²² The jailer put Joseph in charge of all the prisoners, and he became responsible for all that was done there. ²³ The chief jailer did not supervise anything under Joseph's charge because the LORD was with him. And whatever he did, the LORD made it succeed.

Genesis 40
Joseph Interprets the Prisoners' Dreams

¹ Some time later, the king's cupbearer and baker offended him.ᶜ ² Pharaoh was angry with themᵈ ³ so he put them in confinement in the house of the captain of the guard, in the prison where Joseph was confined. ⁴ The captain of the guard put Joseph in charge of them, and he took care of them. They were *kept* in custody for some time.

⁵ The cupbearer and the bakerᵉ had a dream on the same night, and *they realized that* each dream had its own interpretation.

⁶ When Joseph came to them in the morning, he saw that they were frustrated. ⁷ So he asked, "Why are you so sad?"ᶠ

⁸ They answered, "We've each had a dream, but there is no one to interpret them."

Joseph said, "Do not interpretations belong to God? Please, tell me *your dreams.*"

⁹ So the chief cupbearer told his dream to Joseph: "In my dream there was a vine in front of me, ¹⁰ and there were three branches on the vine. It budded, then blossomed, and its clusters produced ripe grapes. ¹¹ Pharaoh's cup was in my hand, so I took the grapes, squeezed them into it, and put it in his hand."

¹² Joseph said, "This is the interpretation: The three branches are three days. ¹³ Within three days Pharaoh will lift up your head and restore you to your office, and you will put Pharaoh's cup in his hand—just as you used to do you were his cupbearer. ¹⁴ But when it goes well with you, please remember me and show me kindness; mention me to Pharaoh and get me out of this prison.ᵍ ¹⁵ I was kidnapped

---

a Literally, "to laugh at us."
b Literally, "the words of his wife."
c Literally, "offended their master, the king of Egypt."
d Literally, "was angry with his two officials, the chief cupbearer and the chief baker."
e Literally, "both men, the king of Egypt's cupbearer and the baker who were confined in the jail."
f Literally, "He saw that they were sad, so he asked Pharaoh's officials who were in confinement in his master's house, 'Why are you so sad.'"
g Literally, "house."

in the land of the Hebrews, and even here I have done nothing to deserve being put into the dungeon."

¹⁶ When the chief baker saw that Joseph had interpreted favorably, he said, "I had a dream too. There were three baskets of bread on my head. ¹⁷ In the top basket there were all kinds of baked goods for Pharaoh, but the birds were eating them out of the basket on my head."

¹⁸ Joseph said to him, "This is the interpretation: The three baskets are three days. ¹⁹ Within three days Pharaoh will lift up your head and hang you from a pole;*a* and the birds will eat your flesh."

²⁰ On the third day, Pharaoh's birthday, he gave a feast for all his officials, and he summoned the chief cupbearer and the chief baker in the presence of his officials. ²¹ He restored the chief cupbearer to his position, and he put the cup into Pharaoh's hand again. ²² But Pharaoh hanged the chief baker just as Joseph had interpreted to them. ²³ The chief cupbearer, however, did not remember Joseph, but forgot him.

Genesis 41
Joseph Interprets Pharaoh's Dreams

¹ Two years later Pharaoh dreamed that he was standing by the Nile ² when seven fine-looking fat cows came out of the river and grazed on the marsh grass. ³ Then seven ugly and gaunt cows came out of the Nile and stood by the others.*b* ⁴ The ugly and gaunt cows ate up the seven fine-looking and fat cows. Then Pharaoh woke up.

⁵ He fell asleep *again* and had a second dream: Seven plump and healthy*c* heads of grain were growing on one stalk. ⁶ Then seven more heads sprouted, thin and scorched by the east wind. ⁷ The thin heads swallowed up the plump and full heads. Then Pharaoh woke up *and realized* it was a dream.

⁸ In the morning his spirit was troubled, so he sent for all the magicians and wise men of Egypt. He told them his dreams, but no one could interpret them to him.

⁹ Then the chief cupbearer said to Pharaoh, "Today I recall my own failures. ¹⁰ Once you were angry with your servants. You imprisoned me and the chief baker in the house of the captain of the guard. ¹¹ One night we each had a dream, and each had its own meaning. ¹² We told our dreams to a young Hebrew, a servant of the captain of the guard who was there with us, and he interpreted them for us.*d* ¹³ And just as he interpreted, so it happened: You restored me to my position, and you hanged*e* the other man."

¹⁴ So Pharaoh sent for Joseph, and they quickly brought him from the dungeon. When he had shaved and changed his clothes, he came to Pharaoh. ¹⁵ And Pharaoh said to Joseph, "I've had a dream no one can interpret. But I have heard it said that when you hear a dream you can interpret it."

---

a   Or "impale you on a pole." And next paragraph.

b   Literally, "by the *other* cows on the bank of the Nile."

c   Literally, "and good."

d   Literally, "he interpreted our dreams for us, giving an interpretation to each one of us according to his own dream."

e   Or "impaled."

¹⁶ "Not me," Joseph replied, "but God will give Pharaoh a favorable answer."

¹⁷ So Pharaoh told Joseph, "In my dream I was standing on the bank of the Nile, ¹⁸ and suddenly seven fine-looking and fat cows came out of the river and grazed on the marsh grass. ¹⁹ Then seven other cows came up, scrawny and very ugly and gaunt. I had never seen such ugly cows in all of Egypt. ²⁰ The lean, ugly cows ate up the seven fat cows *that had come up* first. ²¹ After they ate them, you could not tell that they had eaten. They looked just as ugly as before! Then I woke up.

²² "In my *other* dream I saw seven healthy*a* and plump heads of grain growing on one stalk. ²³ After that, seven *more* heads sprouted, thin and scorched by the east wind. ²⁴ The thin heads swallowed the good heads. I told the magicians, but none could explain *it*."

²⁵ Then Joseph said, "Pharaoh's dreams are one and the same. God has shown Pharaoh what he is about to do. ²⁶ The seven good cows are seven years, and the seven good heads of grain are seven years; the *two* dreams are one. ²⁷ The seven lean, ugly cows that came afterward are seven years, and so are the seven thin heads of grain scorched by the east wind—seven years of famine.

²⁸ "It is *just* as I said: God has shown Pharaoh what he is about to do. ²⁹ Seven years of great abundance are coming throughout all the land of Egypt, ³⁰ after which seven years of famine will come. Famine will ravage the land. ³¹ All the abundance will be forgotten. The *years of* plenty will be unknown throughout Egypt because of the severity of the famine that follows it. ³² As for repeating Pharaoh's dream, the dream was given twice because the matter is firmly established by God—and God will do it soon!

³³ "Now let Pharaoh look for a discerning and wise man and set him over Egypt. ³⁴ Let Pharaoh appoint overseers over the land to exact a fifth of the land of Egypt's *harvest* in the seven years of abundance. ³⁵ Under Pharaoh's authority, let them collect all the food of the good years that are coming and store up the grain in the cities for food. ³⁶ Let them keep it—food as a reserve for the country, for the seven years of famine that will come to Egypt—so that the country will not perish during the famine."

Joseph Put Over Egypt

³⁷ The plan seemed good to Pharaoh and all his officials. ³⁸ So Pharaoh asked them, "Can we find a man like this, *one* in whom is the spirit of God?" ³⁹ Then Pharaoh said to Joseph, "Since God has informed you of all this, *we see that* no one is as discerning and wise as you. ⁴⁰ Therefore, you shall be over my court,*b* and all my people shall submit to your orders. Only *with respect to* the throne will I be greater than you." ⁴¹ And Pharaoh said to Joseph, "I hereby set you over the land of Egypt."

⁴² Then Pharaoh took his signet ring from his hand and put it on Joseph's hand. He dressed him in fine linen and put a gold chain around his neck. ⁴³ He had him ride in a chariot as his second-in-command,*c* and they shouted before him, "Make way!"*d* Thus he set him over the whole land of Egypt.

---

a   Literally, "good."
b   Literally, "palace"; or "house."
c   Or "ride in his second chariot."
d   Literally, "bow the knee."

⁴⁴ Then Pharaoh said to Joseph, "I am Pharaoh; without your *permission* no one will lift hand or foot in all of Egypt." ⁴⁵ Pharaoh then named him Zaphenath-Paneah and gave him Asenath (the daughter of Potiphera, a priest of On) as his wife. ⁴⁶ Joseph was thirty years old when he entered the service of Pharaoh, the king of Egypt, and went out *to rule* over the land of Egypt.

Joseph left Pharaoh's presence and traveled throughout Egypt. ⁴⁷ During the seven years of plenty the land produced abundantly. ⁴⁸ Joseph collected all the food and stored it,^a storing in each city the food grown in its surrounding fields. ⁴⁰ Thus Joseph stored grain in great abundance, like the sand of the sea, until he stopped measuring it because it was beyond measure.

⁵⁰ Before the years of famine came, two sons were born to Joseph. Asenath (the daughter of Potiphera, a priest of On) bore them to him. ⁵¹ Joseph named his firstborn Manasseh (*i.e.,* Made Me Forget) because, he said, "God has made me forget all my trouble and all my father's household." ⁵² The second he named Ephraim (*i.e.,* Made Me Fruitful) "because God has made me fruitful in the land of my suffering."

⁵³⁻⁵⁴ Just as Joseph had said, the seven years of abundance in Egypt came to an end, and seven years of famine began. There was famine in every country. But in Egypt there was food stored up. ⁵⁵ When all Egypt was famished, the people cried out to Pharaoh for food. And he told them, "Go to Joseph and do what he tells you." ⁵⁶ So, after the famine had spread over all the land, Joseph opened all the storehouses and sold to all the Egyptians, for the famine was severe throughout Egypt. ⁵⁷ And all the earth came to Egypt to buy grain from Joseph because the famine was severe in all the lands.

Genesis 42
Joseph's Brothers Go to Egypt

¹ When Jacob saw there was grain in Egypt, he said to his sons, "Why do you *just* keep looking at each other? ² I have heard there is grain in Egypt. Go down there and buy some so that we may live and not die." ³ So Joseph's ten older *half*-brothers went to Egypt to buy grain. ⁴ Jacob did not send Joseph's *full*-brother, Benjamin, because he was thinking, "I'm afraid that harm may befall him." ⁵ So Israel's sons were among those who went to buy grain, for the famine was throughout Canaan also.

⁶ Now Joseph was the ruler over the land, the one who sold *the grain* to all its people. So Joseph's brothers came and bowed down to him with their faces to the ground. ⁷ When Joseph saw his brothers he recognized them, but he pretended he was a stranger and asked harshly, "Where have you come from?"

They replied, "From Canaan, to buy food."

⁸ Though Joseph recognized them, they did not recognize him. ⁹ Then he remembered his dreams about them^b and said, "You are spies! You have come to see *where* the land is unprotected."^c

---

a Literally, "food of those seven years which were in the land of Egypt and put it."

b See Genesis 37:1-11.

c Literally, "is naked."

¹⁰ "No, my lord," they replied. "Your servants have come to buy food. ¹¹ We are all sons of one man. Your servants are honest men, not spies."

¹² But Joseph said, "No! You have come to see where the land is vulnerable."*a*

¹³ And they replied, "Your servants are *just* twelve brothers, the sons of one man in Canaan. The youngest is with our father, and one is no longer alive."*b*

¹⁴ But Joseph persisted, "It is as I said—you are spies! ¹⁵ This is how you will be tested: *I swear* by the life of Pharaoh, you shall not leave this place unless your youngest brother comes here. ¹⁶ Send one of you to get your brother. You shall be confined, to test your words, *to see if* there is truth in you. But if not, by the life of Pharaoh, you are spies." ¹⁷ Then he put them in prison for three days.

¹⁸ On the third day Joseph said to them, "Do this and you will live, for I fear God: ¹⁹ If you are honest men, let one of your brothers be confined in the guardhouse. Then *the rest of* you may go and take grain back *to relieve* the famine of your households. ²⁰ But you must bring your youngest brother to me, so your words can be verified and so that you shall not die." So they agreed.

²¹ They said to one another, "Surely we are guilty concerning our brother. We saw the anguish of his soul when he pleaded with us, but we wouldn't listen. Thus this distress has come upon us."

²² Reuben replied, "Didn't I tell you not to sin against the boy? But you wouldn't listen. Now comes the reckoning for his blood." ²³ They did not know that Joseph understood them, because he had been using an interpreter.*c*

²⁴ Joseph turned away from them and wept. When he returned and spoke to them, he took Simeon and bound him before their eyes. ²⁵ Then Joseph gave orders to fill their bags with grain, to return each man's silver, and to give them provisions for their journey.

Joseph's Brothers Return to Canaan

After this was done for them, ²⁶ they loaded their donkeys with the grain and left. ²⁷ At the lodging place one *of them* opened his sack to give his donkey feed, and he saw money in the mouth of his sack. ²⁸ He called out to his brother, "Look! My money has been returned! It's in my sack!"

Their hearts sank and *they turned* to each other, trembling, wondering aloud, "What is this that God has done to us?" ²⁹ When they came to Jacob in Canaan, they told him all that had happened, saying ³⁰ "The man, the lord of the land, spoke harshly to us and thought we were spying out the country. ³¹ But we said, 'We are honest *men*, not spies. ³² We were twelve brothers, sons of one father. One is no longer alive,*d* and the youngest is with our father in Canaan.' ³³ Then the lord of the land said, 'By this I will know if you are honest men: Leave one of your brothers with me, and take *grain* for the famine of your households and go. ³⁴ But bring your youngest brother to me so I will know that you are honest men, not spies. Then I will give your brother back, and you can trade in the land.'"

---

a Literally, "come to see the nakedness of the land."
b Literally, "one is not."
c Literally, "as there was an interpreter between them."
d Literally, "one is not."

³⁵ *Later,* as they were emptying their sacks, there in each man's sack was his pouch of silver! When they and their father saw the money pouches, they were dismayed.

³⁶ Jacob said, "You have robbed*ᵃ* me of my children. Joseph is no more, and Simeon is no more. And *now* you would take Benjamin *from me?* Everything is against me!"

³⁷ But Reuben replied, "Put both of my sons to death if I do not bring him back to you. Put Benjamin in my care, and I will bring him back."

³⁸ But Jacob said, "My son will not go with you; his brother is dead, and he alone is left. If harm comes to him on the journey you're taking, you will bring my gray head down to Sheol in sorrow."

Genesis 43
Jacob's Sons Go Back to Egypt

¹ Now the famine was still severe in the land. ² And when they had eaten all the grain they had brought from Egypt, their father said to them, "Go back and buy us a little more food."

³ But Judah said, "The man solemnly warned us, 'You shall not see my face unless your brother is with you.' ⁴ If you will send our brother with us, we will go down and buy you food. ⁵ But if you will not send him, we won't go down, because the man said, 'You will not see my face unless your brother is with you.'"

⁶ Israel asked, "Why did you treat me so badly by telling the man you had another brother?"

⁷ They replied, "The man asked directly about us and our family. 'Is your father still alive? Do you have *another* brother?' So we simply answered*ᵇ* his questions. Could we know he'd say, 'Bring your brother down here'?"

⁸ Then Judah suggested to his father Israel, "Send the boy with me and we'll go now,*ᶜ* so we and you and our children can live and not die. ⁹ I myself will guarantee his safety; you can hold me responsible. If I don't bring him back to you,*ᵈ* I will bear the blame before you forever. ¹⁰ If we hadn't delayed, by now we could have gone and returned twice."

¹¹ Then Israel relented, "If *it must be*, then do this: Put some of the best products of the land in your bags and take them to the man as a gift. *Take* balm, honey, spices and myrrh,*ᵉ* pistachio nuts, and almonds. ¹² *Also* take with you*ᶠ* double the money, for you must return the silver that was put back into your sacks.*ᵍ* Perhaps it was an oversight. ¹³ Take your brother and go back at once. ¹⁴ May El Shaddai (*i.e.,* God Almighty) grant you mercy before the man so he will release your other brother and Benjamin. As for me, if *my children* are taken, they are taken."

---

a   Literally, "taken by force."
b   Literally, "answered according to the tenor of."
c   Literally, "arise and go."
d   Literally, "bring him *back* to you and set him before you."
e   "Myrrh": an aromatic tree resin.
f   Literally, "take in your hand."
g   Literally, "into the mouths of the sacks."

¹⁵ So they took Benjamin and the gifts and double the silver, and they departed immediately. ¹⁶ When they presented themselves*ᵃ* to Joseph in Egypt and he saw Benjamin with them, he said to his household steward, "Bring these men to my house. Slay an animal and prepare it for these men, for they are to dine with me at noon." ¹⁷ The man did as Joseph said.*ᵇ*

¹⁸ Now the men were afraid when they were taken to his house, thinking, "We were brought here because of the silver that was put back into our sacks.*ᶜ* He wants to make a case against us and seize us*ᵈ* to make us slaves and take our donkeys."

¹⁹ So they approached Joseph's house steward at the entrance to the house ²⁰ and said, "Please, sir, we came down the first time to buy food, ²² and at the lodging place we opened our sacks and each man's money, the full weight, was in the mouth of his sack. So we have brought it back with us. ²³ We have also brought other money to buy food. We don't know who put our money in the sacks."

²³ He replied, "Peace be to you. Don't be afraid. Your God, the God of your father, has given you treasure in your sacks, for I had your money." ²⁴ Then he brought Simeon out to them, took them into Joseph's house, gave them water to wash their feet, and gave their donkeys feed.

²⁵ Since they had heard they would be eating there, they prepared the gifts for Joseph's arrival at noon. ²⁶ When Joseph came home, they presented their gifts*ᵉ* and bowed down to the ground before him. He asked them about their *family's* welfare, ²⁷ and he asked, "Your aged father, whom you spoke about, is he still alive?"

²⁸ They replied, "Your servant our father is still alive and well." And they bowed low in humility.*ᶠ*

²⁹ When he saw his brother Benjamin, his mother's son, he asked, "Is this your youngest brother of whom you spoke?" Then he said, "God be gracious to you, my son." ³⁰ Overwhelmed with emotion for his brother, Joseph hurried *out* and sought *a place* to weep. He entered his chamber and wept there. ³¹ Then he washed his face and came out. Controlling himself, he ordered, "Serve the meal." ³² They served Joseph by himself, the brothers by themselves, and the Egyptians who ate with them by themselves (because Egyptians could not eat food*ᵍ* with Hebrews, for that is loathsome to Egyptians). ³³ Now they had been seated in front of Joseph *by age:* from the firstborn (as befits his birthright) to the youngest (according to his youth)—and the men looked at each other in astonishment. ³⁴ When portions were served to them from Joseph's table,*ʰ* Benjamin's portion was five times as much as any of theirs. And they drank and got drunk with him.

---

a   Literally, "stood before the face of."
b   Literally, "did as Joseph said and brought them to Joseph's house."
c   Literally, "put into our sacks at the beginning."
d   Literally, "fall upon us."
e   Literally, "the gifts they had brought into the house."
f   Literally, "bowed down and bowed low."
g   Literally, "eat bread."
h   Literally, "when he lifted up to them portions from before his face."

Silver Cup in Benjamin's Sack

¹ Then Joseph ordered his house steward, "Fill the men's sacks with as much food as they can carry, and put each man's money in the mouth of his sack. ² Then put my silver cup in the mouth of the youngest one's sack, along with his money for the grain." So he did.*ᵃ*

³ At dawn the men were sent away with their *loaded* donkeys. ⁴ When they had left the city but were not far away, Joseph ordered his steward, "Get after those men now, and when you overtake them, ask, 'Why have you repaid evil for good? ⁵ Isn't this the cup my master drinks from and uses for divination? You have done evil.'"

⁶ When he overtook them he spoke these same words. ⁷ But they responded, "Why does my lord say such things?*ᵇ* Far be it from your servants to do such a thing! ⁸ Look, we even brought back from Canaan the money we found in the mouth of our sacks. Why then would we steal silver or gold from your master's house? ⁹ If any of us*ᶜ* is found to have it, let him die; and we will be my lord's slaves."

¹⁰ He replied, "Very well,*ᵈ* whoever is found with it will be my slave; *the rest of you* will be *considered* innocent." ¹¹ So each *brother* quickly lowered his sack to the ground and opened it. ¹² They were searched, beginning with the oldest and ending with the youngest. And the cup was found in Benjamin's sack. ¹³ Then each of them tore his clothes*ᵉ* and loaded his donkey, and they returned to the city.

¹⁴ When Judah and his brothers came to Joseph's house, he was still there. So they fell to the ground before him. ¹⁵ Joseph said, "What have you done?*ᶠ* Don't you know that a man like me can learn by divination?"*ᵍ*

¹⁶ Judah answered, "What can we say to my lord? How can we say *anything*? How can we justify ourselves? God has exposed your servants' guilt. We are now my lord's slaves, we ourselves and the one who was found to have the cup."

¹⁷ But Joseph said, "Far be it from me to do such a thing! Only the man who was found to have the cup in his possession*ʰ* will be my slave. The rest of you, go to your father in peace."

Judah Offers Himself

¹⁸ Then Judah approached him and said, "Please, my lord, may your servant speak a word?*ⁱ* Do not be angry with your servant, for I know you are *equal to* Pharaoh. ¹⁹ You, my lord, asked us, your servants, 'Do you have a father or brother?' ²⁰ And we said to you, my lord, 'We have an old father, and *he* has a young son of his old age. The young son's*ʲ* only brother is dead, and he alone is left of *the children* of his mother—and his father loves him.' ²¹ Then you said to your servants, 'Bring him

---

a   Literally, "he did according to the word Joseph had spoken."
b   Literally, "speak such words as these."
c   Literally, "if your servants."
d   Literally, "let it be according to your words."
e   "Tore his clothes": a customary act to create an outward sign of internal anguish.
f   Literally, "what is this deed you have done?"
g   Literally, "can practice divination."
h   Literally, "in his hand."
i   Literally, "speak a word to my lord's ears."
j   Literally, "his."

down to me so I can see him myself."*a* 22 And we said to my lord, 'The boy cannot leave his father. If he leaves him, his father will die.' 23 Then you said, 'Unless your youngest brother comes down with you, you will not see my face again.'

24 "When we went back to your servant my father, we told him what you, my lord, had said.*b* 25 Our father said, 'Go back. Buy a little food.' 26 But we said, 'We cannot go down *without him*. Only if our youngest brother is with us will we go. For we cannot see the man's face unless he is with us.'

27 "Then your servant my father said to us, 'You know that my wife, *Rachel*, bore me two sons. 28 When one disappeared I thought*c* that surely he has been torn to pieces, and I have not seen him since. 29 If you also take this one from me and harm befalls him, you will bring my sorrowful gray-haired *head* down to Sheol.'

30 "So now, if I go to your servant my father, and Benjamin is not with us, since *my father's* life is bound up in his life, 31 when he sees the boy is not with us, he will die. Your servants will bring the gray hair of your servant our father down to Sheol in sorrow. 32 *I myself*, your servant, guaranteed*d* the *safety of* the boy to my father, pledging, 'My father, if I do not bring him back, I will bear the blame before you forever.' 33 Now then, please let your servant remain here as my lord's slave instead of the boy. Let him go with his brothers. 34 How can I go back to my father if the boy is not with me? *If I do, I* will see the misery that will overcome my father."

Genesis 45
Joseph Reveals Himself

1 Then Joseph could not control himself before all his attendants,*e* so he called out, "Have everyone leave me!" Thus none of them were with him when he made himself known to his brothers, 2 but he wept so loudly that the Egyptians heard him—and Pharaoh's household heard about it. 3 He said to his brothers, "I am Joseph! Is my father still living?" But his brothers could not answer because they were terrified at his presence.

4 Then Joseph said to them, "Come closer." And they came closer. He said, "I am your brother Joseph, whom you sold into Egypt. 5 Do not be grieved or angry with yourselves for selling me here, for God sent me here to save lives. 6 For two years there has been famine,*f* and for five more years there will be neither plowing nor reaping. 7 But God sent me ahead of you to preserve your posterity*g* and save your lives by a great deliverance. 8 So it was not you who sent me here, but God. And he has made me an advisor*h* to Pharaoh, lord of all his household, and ruler of all Egypt.

9 "Hurry, go see my father and tell him, 'Joseph, your son, says, "God has made me lord of all Egypt. Come down to me; don't delay. 10 You will live in Goshen and be

---

a Literally, "set my eyes on him."
b Literally, "the words of my lord."
c Literally, "one went out from me I said."
d Literally, "became surety for."
e Literally, "before all those who stood by him."
f Literally, "famine in the land."
g Literally, "preserve a remnant for you."
h Literally, "father."

near me—you, your children and grandchildren, your flocks and herds, and all you have. ¹¹ I will provide for you, for five years of famine are still *to come. Otherwise* you and your household and all that you have will become destitute."'

¹² "Look, your eyes see, and *so do* the eyes of my brother Benjamin, that it is my mouth speaking to you. ¹³ Tell my father about all my glory in Egypt and all that you have seen. And bring my father down here quickly." ¹⁴ Then he fell on Benjamin's neck and wept, and Benjamin wept on his neck. ¹⁵ And he kissed all his brothers and wept upon them, and afterward they talked with him.

¹⁶ When the news that Joseph's brothers had come was heard in Pharaoh's palace, it pleased Pharaoh and all his servants. ¹⁷ Pharaoh told Joseph, "Tell your brothers, 'Do this: Load your animals and return to Canaan. ¹⁸ Bring your father and your households back to me, and I will give you the best land of Egypt and you will eat the fat of the land. ¹⁹ Do this:ᵃ Take wagons from Egypt *to bring back* your children and wives. Get your father and come. ²⁰ Never mind about your goods, for the best of all Egypt is yours.'"

²¹ So the sons of Israel did so. Joseph gave them wagons and provisions for their journey as Pharaoh had commanded. ²² He gave changes of clothing to each, but to Benjamin he gave three hundred *pieces* of silver and five changes of clothes. ²³ He sent his father ten donkeys loaded with the best things of Egypt and ten female donkeys loaded with grain and bread and provisions for the journey *back.* ²⁴ Then he sent his brothers away, and as they departed he said, "Don't quarrel on the way!"

²⁵ So they went up from Egypt and came to their father Jacob in the land of Canaan. ²⁶ They told him, "Joseph is still alive and is ruler of all Egypt!"

²⁷ Jacob was stunned;ᵇ he did not believe them. But when they told him everything Joseph had said, and when he saw the wagons Joseph had sent to carry him, the spirit of their father revived. ²⁸ Then he said, *"I've heard* enough! My son Joseph is still alive. I will go and see him before I die."

Genesis 46
Jacob Moves to Egypt

¹ So Israel set out with all he had. When he reached Beersheba, he offered sacrifices to the God of his father Isaac. ² And God spoke to him in a vision at night. "Jacob! Jacob!" he called.

"Here I am," Jacob replied.

³ "I am God, the God of your father," he said. "Do not be afraid to go down to Egypt, for I will make you into a great nation there. ⁴ I will go down to Egypt with you, and I will surely bring you back again. And Joseph's *hand* will close your eyes."

⁵ Then Jacob left Beersheba, and Israel's sons took him and their children and their wives in the wagons that Pharaoh had sent to carry him. ⁶⁻⁷ They *also* took their livestock and the possessions they had acquired in Canaan. So Jacob and his sons and grandsons and his daughters and granddaughters, all his offspring, went to Egypt. He took all his descendants to Egypt.

---

a   Literally, "You, Joseph, are commanded to say, do this."
b   Literally, "his heart grew numb."

8, 26, 27 These are the names of the Israelites (Jacob and his descendants) who went to Egypt. Sixty-six persons,[b] not counting Jacob's sons' wives. All the persons in Jacob's household who came to Egypt *totalled* seventy (i.e., *the sixty-six* plus *Joseph*, the two sons of Joseph who were with him in Egypt, *and Jacob*).

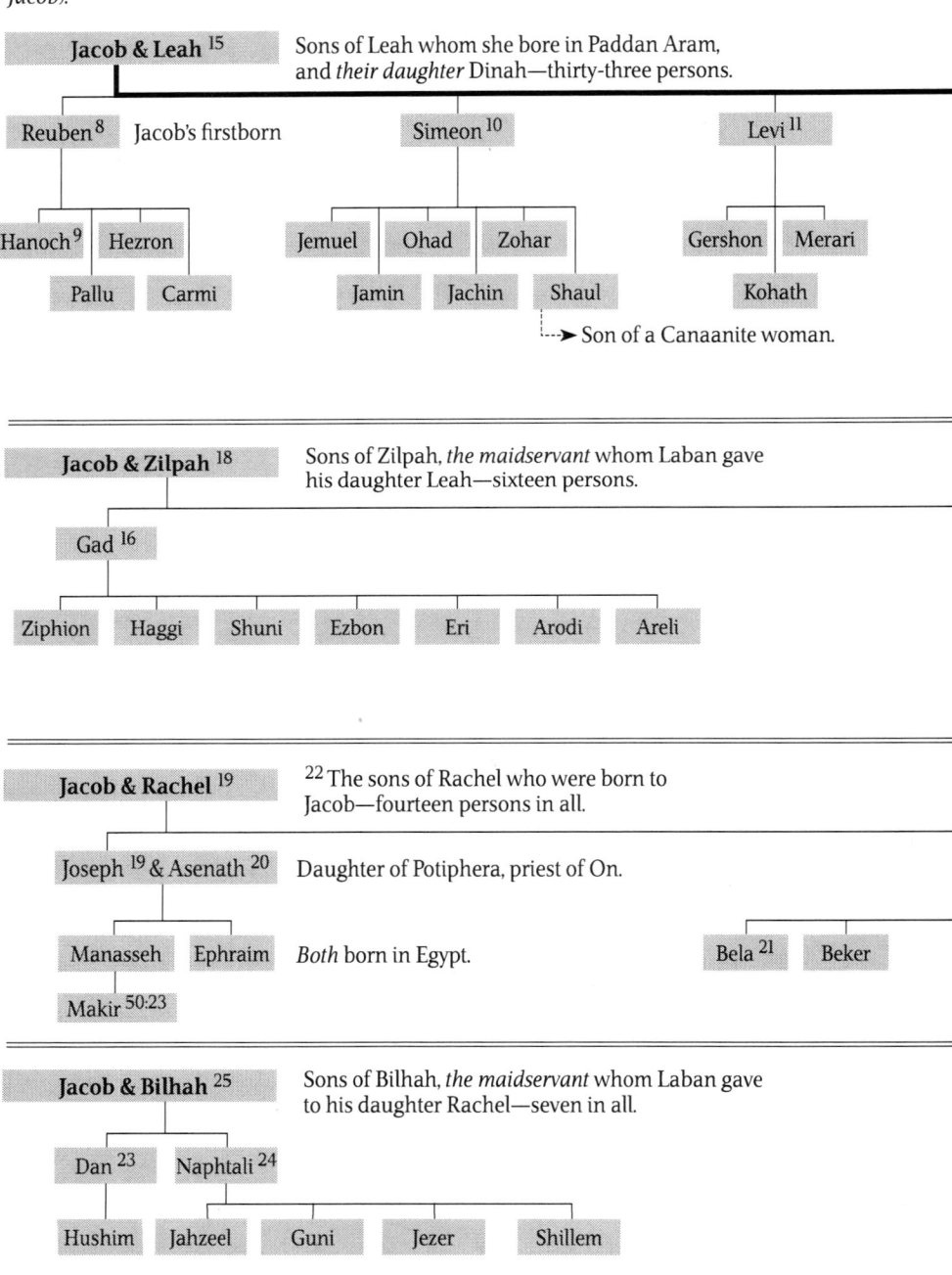

Jacob & Leah [15] — Sons of Leah whom she bore in Paddan Aram, and *their daughter* Dinah—thirty-three persons.

Reuben[8] Jacob's firstborn   Simeon[10]   Levi[11]

Hanoch[9] Hezron   Jemuel Ohad Zohar   Gershon Merari

Pallu Carmi   Jamin Jachin Shaul   Kohath

➤ Son of a Canaanite woman.

Jacob & Zilpah [18] — Sons of Zilpah, *the maidservant* whom Laban gave his daughter Leah—sixteen persons.

Gad [16]

Ziphion Haggi Shuni Ezbon Eri Arodi Areli

Jacob & Rachel [19] — [22] The sons of Rachel who were born to Jacob—fourteen persons in all.

Joseph [19] & Asenath [20] Daughter of Potiphera, priest of On.

Manasseh Ephraim *Both* born in Egypt.   Bela [21] Beker

Makir [50:23]

Jacob & Bilhah [25] — Sons of Bilhah, *the maidservant* whom Laban gave to his daughter Rachel—seven in all.

Dan [23] Naphtali [24]

Hushim Jahzeel Guni Jezer Shillem

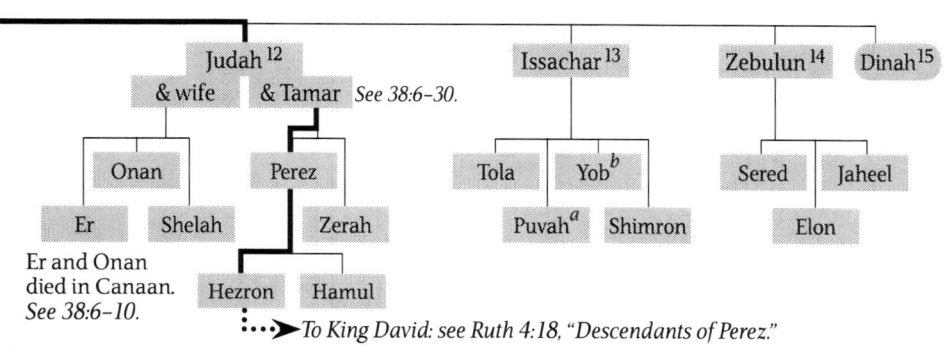

Judah [12]
& wife   & Tamar   *See 38:6-30.*

Onan   Perez

Er   Shelah   Zerah

Er and Onan
died in Canaan.   Hezron   Hamul
See 38:6-10.

⋯▶*To King David: see Ruth 4:18, "Descendants of Perez."*

Issachar [13]

Tola   Yob[b]

Puvah[a]   Shimron

Zebulun [14]   Dinah[15]

Sered   Jaheel

Elon

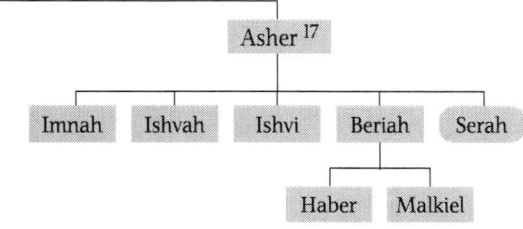

Asher [17]

Imnah   Ishvah   Ishvi   Beriah   Serah

Haber   Malkiel

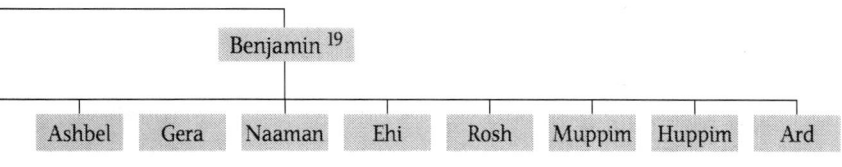

Benjamin [19]

Ashbel   Gera   Naaman   Ehi   Rosh   Muppim   Huppim   Ard

---

a   "See also, "Jacob's sons": Gen. 35:23.

b   "66 persons": all his sons and grandsons less Joseph and his two sons (who were already in
    Egypt). Some of Jacob's grandchildren were born in Egypt. For instance, Reuben had four sons
    in total but only had two before going to Egypt (see 42:37).

c   Some manuscripts, "Puah."

d   Some manuscripts, "Jashub."

^{28} Now Jacob sent Judah ahead of him to Joseph *so he could* point out the way^a to Goshen. When they arrived there, ^{29} Joseph prepared his chariot and went to meet his father Israel. As soon as Joseph appeared before him, he hugged his neck and wept on it for a long time. ^{30} Israel told him, "Now I am ready to die, since I have seen your face *and know* you are still alive."

^{31} Then Joseph told his brothers and his father's household, "I will go and tell Pharaoh, 'My brothers and my father's household, who were in Canaan, have come to me, ^{32} and the men are shepherds. They keep livestock, and they have brought along their flocks and herds and all they have.' ^{33} When Pharaoh calls for you and asks, 'What is your occupation?' ^{34} tell him, 'Your servants, like our ancestors, have tended livestock from our youth until now,' in order that you may live in Goshen, for shepherds are repugnant to the Egyptians."

Genesis 47

^{1} Joseph went and told Pharaoh, "My father and brothers, with their flocks and herds and everything they own, have come from Canaan and are now in Goshen." He chose five of his brothers^b and presented them to Pharaoh.

^{3} Pharaoh asked the brothers, "What is your occupation?"

They replied to Pharaoh, "Your servants, like our ancestors, are shepherds. ^{4} We have come to live here temporarily because the famine is severe in Canaan and there is no pasture for your servants' flocks. So now, please let your servants live in Goshen."

^{5} Pharaoh said to Joseph, "Your father and your brothers have come to you. ^{6} The land of Egypt is before you; settle your father and your brothers on the best land. Let them live in Goshen. And if you know of any capable men among them, put them in charge of my livestock."

^{7} Then Joseph brought in his father and presented Jacob before Pharaoh. After Jacob blessed Pharaoh, ^{8} Pharaoh asked him, "How old are you?"

^{9} Jacob replied to Pharaoh, "The years of my temporary residing on earth^c have been few and unpleasant, a hundred and thirty, not equal to the lives of my fathers."^{d} ^{10} Then Jacob blessed Pharaoh and left.^{e}

^{11} So Joseph settled his father and his brothers and gave them property^f in the best *part* of Egypt, the land of Rameses, as Pharaoh ordered. ^{12} Joseph also provided them, and everyone in his father's household, with food according to the number of their children.

---

a Literally, "direct his face."
b Literally, "he took five men from among his brothers."
c Or "of my pilgrimage."
d Literally, "not up to the days of the years of the life of my fathers in their days of sojourning."
e Literally, "and went out from his presence."
f Literally, "gave them a possession."

¹³ Now there was no food throughout the land because the famine was so severe. Egypt and Canaan wasted away because of it. ¹⁴ Joseph collected and brought to Pharaoh's house all the money to be found in Egypt and Canaan *as payment* for the grain the people*ᵃ* purchased. ¹⁵ When all the money *of the people* of Egypt and Canaan was spent, all the Egyptians came to Joseph and said, "Give us food. Why should we die in your presence? Our money is gone."

¹⁶ Joseph answered, "Since your money is gone, bring your livestock and I will give you food in exchange for your livestock." ¹⁷ So they brought their livestock to him, and he gave them food in exchange for horses, flocks, herds, and donkeys. Thus that year Joseph fed them with food in exchange for all their livestock.

¹⁸ When that year was over, they came to him the next year and said, "We cannot hide from my lord that our money is gone and our livestock are my lord's. There is nothing left in the sight of our lord except our bodies and our land. ¹⁹ Why should we die before your eyes, both we and our land? Buy us and our land for food, and we and our land will be slaves to Pharaoh. Give us grain*ᵇ* that we may live and not die, and that the land may not become desolate."

²⁰ So Joseph bought all the land of Egypt for Pharaoh. All the Egyptians sold their land because the famine was so hard on them. Thus the land became Pharaoh's, ²¹ and he made all the people slaves.*ᶜ* ²² However, he did not buy the priests' land, because they had an allowance*ᵈ* from Pharaoh and lived on it. So they did not sell their land.

²³ Then Joseph said to the people, "Now that I have bought you and your land for Pharaoh, here's seed for you to sow.*ᵉ* ²⁴ But when you harvest, you must give a fifth to Pharaoh and keep four-fifths as your own, as seed for the fields and as food for your families."*ᶠ*

²⁵ The people responded, "You have saved our lives. May we find favor in the sight of our lord. We will be Pharaoh's slaves."*ᵍ*

²⁶ So Joseph made it a statute *valid even* to this day throughout Egypt, that Pharaoh gets a fifth. Only the priests' land did not became Pharaoh's.

Jacob's Burial Request

²⁷ Now the Israelites settled in Egypt in Goshen. They acquired property there and were fruitful and increased greatly in number. ²⁸ Jacob lived there seventeen years, until he was 147 years old.*ʰ* ²⁹ When the time drew near for him to die, he called Joseph and said, "If I have found favor in your sight, put your hand under my

---

a   Literally, "they."

b   Or "seed."

c   The Hebrew is not clear. "Made all the people slaves" is the Septuagint and Samaritan Pentateuch translation. The text seems to say, "he moved the people town by town," or, "he removed them to the cities." Thus, he took them off their ancestral land holdings.

d   Or "a portion."

e   Literally, "to sow the ground."

f   Literally, "for yourselves and your households and your little ones."

g   Or "servants."

h   Literally, "and the length of years of Jacob's life was 147 years."

thigh and *pledge* to deal with me with kindness and faithfulness. Please do not bury me in Egypt, ³⁰ but when I lie with my fathers, carry me out of Egypt and bury me where they are buried."

Joseph replied, "I will do as you have asked."

³¹ Israel said, "Swear to me." Then he swore to him. Then Israel worshiped *the Lord*[a] at the head of his bed.

Genesis 48
Jacob Adopts Manasseh and Ephraim

¹ Sometime later Joseph was told, "Your father is sick." So he took his two sons Manasseh and Ephraim with him.

² When Jacob was told, "Your son Joseph has come," Israel gathered his strength and sat up on the bed ³ and told Joseph, "God Almighty appeared to me in Canaan at Luz. There he blessed me ⁴ and said, 'I will make you fruitful and many. I will make you a community of peoples, and I will give this land *of Canaan* as an everlasting possession to your descendants after you.' ⁵ Now, your two sons who were born in Egypt before I came to Egypt will be mine. Ephraim and Manasseh will be mine just as Reuben and Simeon are mine. ⁶ Your offspring after them will be yours, but their inheritance is to be listed under their brothers' names.[b] ⁷ Now as for me, when I came from Paddan *Aram*, to my sorrow Rachel died in Canaan while we were still some distance from Ephrath (that is, Bethlehem). So I buried her there beside the road to Ephrath."[c]

⁸ When Israel saw Joseph's sons, he asked, "Who are these?"

⁹ Joseph said, "They are the sons God has given me here."

So he said, "Bring them to me so I may bless them."

¹⁰ Now Israel's eyes were so dim from age that he could not see *well*. So Joseph brought them close, and Israel kissed them and embraced them. ¹¹ He told Joseph, "I never expected to see your face, and now God has allowed me to see your children too."

¹² Then Joseph moved aside the boys (who were at Israel's knees) and bowed before him with his face to the ground. ¹³ Then Joseph placed Ephraim on his right (toward Israel's left hand) and Manasseh on his left (toward Israel's right hand), and brought them close to Israel. ¹⁴ But Israel, crossing his hands, stretched out his right and put it on Ephraim's head (though he was younger) and put his left on Manasseh's head (even though he was the firstborn).

---

a Literally, "bowed down."

b Literally, "be called by their brothers' names." Thus, Ephraim and Manasseh were elevated to tribal status. Thus, any land owned by other children of Joseph will be in Ephraim's or Manasseh's tribal allocation.

c See Genesis 35:16ff.

¹⁵ *First* he blessed Joseph:

"God,

> Before whom my fathers Abraham and Isaac walked.

God who has been

> My shepherd all my life to this day,

¹⁶ The angel who has delivered me from all evil;

Bless these boys.

Let my name and the names of my fathers Abraham and Isaac live on in them.

May they grow into a multitude upon the earth."

¹⁷ When Joseph saw his father lay his right hand on Ephraim's head he was not pleased. So he grasped it to move it from Ephraim's head to Manasseh's head ¹⁷ and said to his father, "Not like that, Father; this one is the firstborn. Place your right hand on his head."

¹⁹ But his father refused: "I know, my son, I know. He too will become a people and become great. Nevertheless, his younger brother will be greater than he, and his descendants will become a multitude of nations." ²⁰ So he blessed them that day:

> *"In the future,* Israel will pronounce blessings *using* your names,[a] *saying,*

> > 'May God make you *as prosperous* as Ephraim and Manasseh.'"

Thus Israel put Ephraim ahead of Manasseh.

²¹ Then Israel said to Joseph, "Look, I am about to die, but God will be with you and take you back to the land of your ancestors. ²² And I have given to you one portion *of land* more than your brothers, of the land I took from the Amorites with my sword and bow."

Genesis 49
Jacob Blesses His Sons

¹ Jacob called his sons and said, ² "Gather around so I can tell you what will happen to you in days to come. Come together and listen, sons of Jacob; listen to your father Israel:

³ **Reuben**, you are

> My firstborn,
> My might,
> The first sign of my strength,
> Prevailing in rank,
> Prevailing in power,

⁴ Uncontrollable[b] as the waters.

> You will no longer prevail,[c] for you went up to your father's bed—to my couch—and defiled it![d]

---

a   Literally, "pronounce blessings by you."

b   Or "unstable."

c   Literally, "excel." Perhaps a reference to his losing the privileges of the firstborn son.

d   See Genesis 35:22.

⁵ **Simeon** and **Levi**:

> Two of a kind;^{a}
> Their swords are instruments of violence.^{b}
> May I^c never participate in their meetings;^{d}
> May my heart^e never be united with that group;
>> For in their anger they have killed men—even hamstrung^f oxen for delight!

> ⁵ Cursed be their anger for its fierceness;
> *Cursed be* their wrath for its cruelness!
> I will scatter them amongst *the families of* Jacob and disperse them throughout Israel.

⁸ **Judah,**

> Your brothers will praise you;
> Your hands will be on the necks of your enemies;
> Your father's sons will bow down to you.
>> ⁹ Judah is a lion's cub.
>> He, my son, returns from eating his prey;
>> Then he crouches and lies down like a lion or a lioness,
>>> Who would to rouse him?

> ¹⁰ The scepter^g will not depart from Judah,
> Nor the ruler's staff from between his feet
> *That is*
>> Until he to whom it belongs comes^h and the obedience of the nations is his.
>>> ¹¹ He will tie his donkey to a vine—his donkey's colt to a choice vine. He will wash his garments in wine and his robes in the blood of grapes.
>>> ¹² His eyes will be darker than wine, his teeth whiter than milk.

¹³ **Zebulun**

> Will live by the seashore and have a haven for ships.
> His border will be toward Sidon.

---

a Literally, "brothers."

b Or "their knives are weapons of violence." Perhaps a reference to their circumcision knives and the slaughter in Genesis 34.

c Or "my soul."

d Literally, "join their council."

e Literally, "glory."

f "Hamstrung": cut the leg tendon (the hamstring) so that an animal cannot walk.

g "Scepter": a ceremonial staff signifying royalty.

h The Hebrew of this line is not clear. Instead of translating the Hebrew word *shilo* (which we render as "to whom it belongs"), some translations transliterate it, rendering "until Shiloh comes, and…"

¹⁴ **Issachar**

Is a strong donkey lying down between hearths.^{*a*}

¹⁵ When he sees his resting place is good and the land is pleasant,
He will bow his shoulder to bear *a burden* and become a slave laborer.

¹⁶ **Dan**

Will judge his people as one of Israel's tribes,
¹⁷ Will be a serpent by the road, a horned snake along the path that bites the horse's heels so that its rider falls backward.
¹⁸ (I look for your salvation, O LORD.)

¹⁹ **Gad** will be attacked by raiders, but he will attack them in their retreat.^{*b*}

²⁰ **Asher** will have rich food. He will provide royal delicacies.

²¹ **Naphtali** is a doe set free that utters beautiful words.^{*c*}

²² **Joseph,**

Is a fruitful vine near a spring, a fruitful vine whose branches run over a wall.^{*d*}
²³ Archers bitterly attacked him, shot at him, and harassed him,
²⁴ But

His bow remained steady,
His strong hands stayed agile,

Because of^{*e*} the hands of the Mighty One of Jacob;
Because of the Shepherd, the Rock of Israel;
²⁵ Because of the God of your father, who helps you;
Because of God Almighty who blesses you

With blessings of heaven above,
With blessings of the deep that lies below,
With blessings of the breast and womb.

²⁶ Your father's blessings have surpassed the blessings of my ancestors and the bounty of the age-old hills.
May they rest upon the head of Joseph, on the brow of the prince among his brothers.

²⁷ **Benjamin** is a ravenous wolf.

In the morning he devours his prey.
In the evening he divides his spoil.

²⁸ These men are the twelve tribes of Israel, and this is what their father said to them when he blessed them, giving each the blessing appropriate to him.

---

a   Or "between sheep pens"; or "between saddlebags." The Hebrew is not clear.
b   Literally, "at their heels."
c   Or "that bears beautiful fawns." The Hebrew is not clear.
d   Perhaps a reference to his sons seeking to increase their territory (see Joshua 17:14–18).
e   Or "by the." And the following three occurrences.

The Death of Jacob

29,32 Then he charged them: "I am about to die.*a* Bury me with my fathers in the cave in the field brought from Ephron the Hittite.*b* 30 *That is,* the burial site in the field of Machpelah, near Mamre in Canaan, which Abraham bought with a field from Ephron the Hittite. 31 That's where they buried Abraham and his wife Sarah, and Isaac and his wife Rebekah. And I buried Leah there."*c*

33 When Jacob finished charging his sons, he drew his feet into the bed and breathed his last and was gathered to his people.

Genesis 50
Jacob's Burial

1 Joseph fell on his father's face, wept over him, and kissed him. 2 Then he directed the physicians in his service to embalm him (3 which they did *over* the forty days required for embalming).*d* And the Egyptians wept for him for seventy days.

4 When the days of mourning were past, Joseph said to Pharaoh's advisors,*e* "If I have found favor in your sight, please speak to Pharaoh *for me.* Tell him that 5 my father made me swear, saying, 'I am about to die. Bury me in the tomb I hewed out for myself in Canaan. Bury me there.' Please let me go now and bury my father. Then I will return."

6 And Pharaoh said, "Go up and bury your father as he made you swear."

7 So Joseph went to bury his father with all Pharaoh's officials*f*—the elders of his court and all the elders of the land of Egypt— 8 *as well as* all the members of Joseph's and his brothers' and father's household. Only their children and flocks and herds were left in Goshen. 9 Chariots and horsemen went too. It was a very large group.

10 When they reached the threshing floor of Atad beyond the Jordan, they mourned with a great and sorrowful lamentation, and Joseph observed seven days of mourning. 11 When the inhabitants of the land, the Canaanites, saw the mourning on the threshing floor of Atad, they said, "The Egyptians are mourning grievously." That is why that place near the Jordan is called Abel Mizraim (*i.e.,* Mourning of the Egyptians).

12 So Jacob's sons did as he had commanded them: 13 They carried him to Canaan and buried him in the cave in the field of Machpelah.*g* 14 After burying him, Joseph and all who had gone with him to bury his father returned to Egypt.

---

a   Literally, "be gathered to my people."
b   See Genesis 23.
c   Literally, "I buried Leah in the field and the cave that is in it bought from the sons of Heth."
d   Literally, "so the physicians embalmed Israel for the forty days that were required for it, for such is the period required for embalming."
e   Literally, "household."
f   Literally, "servants."
g   Literally, "the cave in the field of Machpelah which Abraham had bought with the field from Ephron the Hittite as a burial site."

Joseph's Continuing Forgiveness

15 When Joseph's brothers saw that their father was dead, they worried, "What if Joseph holds a grudge against us and pays us back for all the wrongs we did to him?" 16 So they sent *this message* to him: "Your father instructed us before he died, 17 'Tell Joseph, "I ask you, please forgive your brothers for their transgression, their sin, the evil they committed against you."'

Now please forgive the sins of *us*, the servants of the God of your father." Joseph wept when he received the message.*a* 18 Then his brothers threw themselves down before him and declared, "We are your slaves."

19 But Joseph said, "Don't be afraid. Am I in God's place? 20 As for you, you meant evil against me, but God intended it for good. He brought about this present result to save the lives of many people, just as it is being done today.*b* 21 So then, don't be afraid. I will provide for you and your children." And he comforted them and spoke kindly to them.

The Death of Joseph

22 Joseph and his father's household stayed in Egypt. He lived a hundred and ten years 23 and saw the third generation of Ephraim's children. The sons of Manasseh's son, Makir, were placed on Joseph's knees at their birth.*c*

24 *One day* Joseph told his brothers, "I am about to die. But God will surely care for you and take you up from this land to the land he promised with an oath to Abraham, Isaac, and Jacob." 25 Then Joseph made the sons of Israel swear, "God will surely take care of you, and you will carry my bones up from this place."

26 So Joseph died at the age of a hundred and ten, and he was embalmed and placed in a coffin in Egypt.

s

---

a Literally, "when they spoke."
b Literally, "as this day."
c Literally, "were born on Joseph's knees."

Genesis Glossary

The Readable Bible uses the same words that we use in everyday conversation as much as possible. Words that are not used in secular life or that are used but commonly misunderstood are defined in footnotes if they are only used once or twice, in the Glossary if they are used more often.

Bless, blessed	God toward people: to watch over, protect, bestow holiness upon (e.g., "God will bless us").
	People toward God: to declare approval and support. To praise and/or honor (e.g., "I will bless the Lord").
	People toward people: to call upon God for his care of someone (e.g., "May God bless you").
Bowed down	The exact action is uncertain. It may be that the person dropped to their knees and put their head on the ground, or dropped to a knee and bowed their head. Whatever the act, it was the normal gesture by which one acknowledges the lordship of the person before them.
Burnt offering	See "Sacrifice."
Called upon the name of the Lord	Perhpas an idom meaning "worship the Lord."
Canaan	Roughly, today's Lebanon, Israel, Palestinian territories, the western part of Jordan and southwestern Syria. The exact borders are given in Numbers 34:3–12. However, some of the locations cited are uncertain.
City	Cities in Canaan in the second millennium BC were seldom larger than five thousand people, and typically much smaller. Generally, we use "town" only for very small communities.
City gate	Since the city gate controlled who could enter or leave, and since it was where officials met the people and where the residents gathered, the term became a symbol for control of the city.
Covenant	A solemn agreement, either mutually agreed to or imposed by God, that binds the parties to one another in a permanent, defined relationship. It may include promises, claims, and/or obligations. Some covenants were "cut" by each party walking between the two halves of a slain animal and calling down upon themselves the fate of the animal if they violated the agreement.
Divination	Getting information by occult ritual.
Fear	With reference to God, regard with deep reverence, respect, and awe. For the believer, it does not include a sense of anxiety or dread.
Foreigner	Usually a translation of "ger," traditionally translated "sojourner." Depending upon the context, we render "foreigner" or "stranger."
King	A king was the ruler over a city and its surrounding territory, which would sometimes have been a relatively small area (see "city" above).
Lord	The name of God is four Hebrew letters represented in English by YHWH. Out of reverence for God's name, we usually render the word as "Lord." When the context calls for God's actual name, we supply the vowels and render it as "Yahweh" (pronounced "Yah-weh").
	The Hebrew, YHWH, may be translated "He who is," "He who exists," "He who causes to exist," or "He who gives life." French Bible translations render YHWH as *L'Eternel* (i.e., "The Eternal").

Lord, my lord	Terms of respect used by a person of lower rank when addressing a person of higher rank.
LORD GOD LORD MY God Sovereign LORD	When "Yahweh" appears after *adonai* (a Hebrew term of reverence for God), we usually render the two words as "Lord GOD." However, since these are two synonymous terms next to each other, one reinforcing the other, they can equally well be rendered "Sovereign LORD." The Readable Bible rendering depends upon the context.
Lovingkindness	A steadfast, faithful, and loyal love full of kindness and mercy. .
Negev	A dry, mostly mountainous region ranging from the dunes of the Mediterranean to the Dead Sea valley, from between Hebron and Beersheba south to its apex at Eilat on the Gulf of Aqaba. Though called a desert, it has areas of fertile soil with a foot of rainfall. The term, from the Hebrew root meaning "dry," can also denote "south."
Offering	See "Sacrifice."
Paddan Aram	Upper Mesopotamia, the area above where the Harbur River joins the Euphrates River.
Pillar	A pile of stones, usually set up as a memorial.
Princes	Tribal rulers, leaders; not necessarily sons of a king.
Rules	Rules, regulations, and stipulations are terms for actions that are either required or forbidden by God. Other common terms in English translations include: decrees, judgements, laws, ordinances, and statutes. The terms appear synonymous, though some scholars would argue there is a difference. However, since the differences are not clear (and thus, their use provides little, if any, benefit to the reader), we use the terms interchangeably.
Sacrifice	A gift/offering to God, oftentimes presented by burning it. It was offered to express appreciation for what God had done for the offeror or to appease him for the offeror's sin. See Leviticus 1–7. The owner makes the offering as an act of faith, believing that the Lord will accept it as an outward sign of their inward belief in him, acceptance of his lordship, and desire to be in harmonious relationship with him.
Seir	The country around Mt. Seir, southeast of the Dead Sea.
Shall	"Shall," "is/are to," and "must" are used to indicate a command, or to emphatically state a fact (e.g., "The Lord shall reign forever"). "Will" is used to point to a future event or condition.
Sheol	The place of the dead who are not with God. Sometimes it refers to a person's grave, or to death in general.
Soul	The Hebrew term *nephesh* refers to the non-physical part of personhood. It may also be rendered as a personal pronoun. For example, "*nephesh* sings" can be rendered, "my soul sings" or "I sing."
Stranger	See "Foreigner."
Wilderness	An uninhabited area with desert-like characteristics, though not necessarily sandy. Sometimes mountainous, often with terraces and steep cliffs from high lands to ravines over a thousand feet below.

Familiar Verses in Genesis[a]

1:1	In the beginning God created the heavens and the earth.
1:26	Then he said, "Let us make man in our own image, in our own likeness, and let them rule over the fish of the sea, the birds of the air, the livestock, and all the wild animals—over all the earth."
1:27	So God created human beings in his own image. In the image of God he created them. And he created them male and female.
1:28	God blessed them and said to them, "Be fruitful and multiply in number; fill the earth and subdue it."
2:3	And God blessed the seventh day and made it holy because on it he rested from all he had been doing, the work of creation.
2:7	The Lord God formed man from the dust of the earth and breathed into his nostrils the breath of life, and the man became a living being.
2:8	The Lord God had planted a garden in the east, in Eden, and he put the man he had formed there.
2:16-17	[16] And the Lord God warned the man, "Eat freely from any tree in the garden, [17] but you must not eat from the tree of knowledge of good and evil, for on the day you eat from it you will surely die."
2:18	Then the Lord God said, "It is not good for the man to be alone. I will make him a helper to be alongside him."
2:21-22	[21] While he slept, God took one of Adam's ribs and then closed up the flesh. [22] Then the Lord God made a woman from the rib taken from the man.
2:23-24	[23] The man said, "This now is bone of my bones and flesh of my flesh. She shall be called 'woman' because she was taken out of man." [24] That is why a man leaves his father and mother and bonds with his wife— and they become one flesh.
3:6-7	[6] When she saw that the fruit of the tree was good for food and a delight to the eyes, and also desirable to make one wise, she took some of its fruit and ate it. She also gave some to her husband, who was with her, and he ate. [7] Then the eyes of both of them were opened, and they realized they were naked; so they sewed fig leaves together to make themselves loincloths.
3:14	*To the serpent:* "Because you have done this, cursed are you above all the livestock and all the wild animals. You will crawl on your belly and eat dust all the days of your life."
3:16	I will greatly increase your pain in childbearing; in pain you will give birth to children. Your desire will be for your husband, and he will rule over you.
3:17	Because you listened to your wife and ate from the tree about which I warned you (when I said 'You shall not eat from it'), the ground is cursed because of you.
3:19	By the sweat of your brow will you eat your food until you return to the ground—because from it you were taken, for you are made from dust and to dust you will return.

---

a   The formatting and punctuation of some of the verses below differs from that in the body of the book.

3:23	So the LORD God sent him from the Garden of Eden to work the ground from which he had been taken.
4:7b	Sin is crouching at the door, and it desires to have you, but you must master it.
4:9	Then the LORD asked Cain, "Where is your brother, Abel?" He replied, "I don't know. Am I my brother's keeper?"
6:5	The LORD saw how great man's wickedness had become on the earth—that every thought of his heart was always inclined toward evil.
8:21–22	[21] When the LORD smelled the pleasing aroma, he said in his heart, "Never again will I curse the ground because of man, even though every intent of his heart is evil from his youth. And never again will I destroy every living creature as I have done. [22] As long as the earth remains, seedtime and harvest, cold and heat, summer and winter, and day and night will not cease."
9:13–16	[13] I will place my rainbow in the clouds, and it will be the sign of my covenant between you and me. [14] Whenever I bring clouds over the earth and the rainbow is seen in the clouds, [15] I will remember my covenant between me and you and every living creature—all flesh. Never again will the waters become a flood to destroy all flesh. [16] I will see it when the rainbow is in the clouds, and I will remember the everlasting covenant between God and every kind of living creature—all flesh on earth.
12:1–3	[1] The LORD said to Abram, "Leave your country, your people, and your father's house, and go to the land that I will show you. [2] I will make you into a great nation, and I will bless you and make your name great. You will be a blessing, [3] and I will bless those who bless you and curse those who curse you. And through you all the peoples on earth will be blessed."
13:14–16	[14] The LORD said to Abram after Lot had departed, "Lift up your eyes and look to the north and south and to the east and west. [15] I will give you and your descendants forever all the land that you see. [16] I will make your descendants like the dust of the earth, so that if anyone could count the earth's dust particles, then your descendants could also be counted."
15:5–6	[5] God took him outside and said, "Look toward the heavens and count the stars—if you are able to count them. That's how many descendants you will have." [6] Abram believed the LORD, and God counted him as righteous because of his faith.
17:4b–8	[4b] You will be the father of many nations. [5] You will no longer be called Abram (i.e., Exalted Father), but your name will be Abraham (i.e., Father of Many) for I have made you a father of many nations. [6] I will make you exceedingly fruitful. I will make nations of you, and kings will come forth from you. [7] I will establish my covenant as an everlasting covenant between me and you and your descendants, to be your God and the God of your descendants after you. [8] I will give you and your descendants forever the whole land of Canaan, where you are now living as foreigners, as an everlasting possession. And I will be their God.
17:10	This is my covenant with you and your descendants, the covenant you are to keep: Every male among you is to be circumcised.
18:14a	Is anything too hard for the LORD?

18:19	For I have chosen him, that he will command his children and his household after him to keep the way of the LORD by doing righteousness and justice, so that I will bring about for Abraham what I promised.
18:20	The outcry of Sodom and Gomorrah is so great, and their sin is so exceedingly grave.
18:23, 32	23 Then Abraham approached him and asked, "Will you sweep away the righteous with the wicked?" 32 Then he said, "Lord, don't be angry, but let me speak just one more time. What if only 10 can be found there?" He answered, "For the sake of 10, I will not destroy it."
22:8a	Abraham answered, "God himself will provide the lamb for the burnt offering, my son."
22:14	Abraham called the name of that place Yahweh Yireh (i.e., The LORD Will Provide), and it is still said, "On the mountain of the LORD it will be provided."
22:16–18	16 I myself swear, declares the LORD, that because you have done this and have not withheld your son, your only son, 17 I will certainly bless you, and I will multiply your descendants enormously—as the stars of the heavens and as the sand of the seashore. And your descendants shall take possession of their enemies' cities. 18 And through your descendants all the nations on earth will be blessed because you have obeyed my voice.
23:17–19	17 The LORD thought, "Shall I hide from Abraham what I am about to do? 18 For he will surely become a great and powerful nation, and all nations will be blessed through him. 19 For I have chosen him, that he will command his children and his household after him to keep the way of the LORD by doing righteousness and justice, so that I will bring about for Abraham what I promised.
26:3–5	3 Settle in the land I will tell you about. Live as foreigners in this land, and I will be with you and will bless you. For to you and your descendants - I will give all these lands; - I will establish the oath I swore to your father, Abraham, 4 and - I will make your descendants as numerous as the stars of heaven. I will give them all these lands, and through your descendants all nations on earth shall be blessed 5 because Abraham obeyed me and kept my charge, my commandments, my rules, and my regulations.
28:13–14	13 The LORD stood above it and said, "I am the LORD, the God of your father Abraham and the God of Isaac. I will give you and your descendants the land on which you lie. 14 Your descendants will be like the dust of the earth, and you will spread out to the north, east, south, and west. All peoples on earth will be blessed through you and your offspring."
45:7–8	7 But God sent me ahead of you to preserve your posterity and save your lives by a great deliverance. 8 So it was not you who sent me here, but God. And he has made me an advisor to Pharaoh, lord of all his household, and ruler of all Egypt.
50:20–21	20 "As for you, you meant evil against me, but God intended it for good. He brought about this present result to save the lives of many people, just as it is being done today. 21 So then, don't be afraid. I will provide for you and your children." And he comforted them and spoke kindly to them.

Overlapping Lives of the Patriarchs

Italicized numbers are calculated, not in the biblical text.

Genesis Reference	Age				Event
	Abram	Isaac	Jacob	Joseph	
11:26, 31	0				Terah moves his family from Ur of the Chaldeans to Haran.
12:1–4					The call of Abraham. He moves to Shechem.
12:8					Abraham moves to between Bethel and Ai.
12:10					Abraham moves to Egypt because of famine.
12:13					Abraham tells Pharaoh that Sarah is his sister.
13:1–2					Abraham moves to the Negev.
13:3	75				Abraham moves back between Bethel and Ai.
13:9–11					Lot moves to Sodom after Abraham gives him first choice of the land.
14:13–16					Abraham defeats the northern kings and rescues Lot.
14:17–20					Abraham pays a tithe to Melchizedek.
15:1–20					God makes a covenant with Abraham, promising him land and many descendants, and foretelling the Israelites' Egyptian bondage and release.
15:6					Abraham believes God's promise to make him a great nation, and it is counted as righteousness.
16:1–7	86				Ishmael is conceived. Hagar flees to Shur.
16:8–16	86				God promises Hagar children beyond number. She returns, and Ishmael is born.
17:5	99				God changes Abram's name to "Abraham" and says nations will descend from him.
17:10	99				God gives the circumcision covenant to Abraham.
18:10	99				God foretells Isaac's birth.
18:23–32	99				Abraham pleads for the righteous people who live in Sodom.
19:23–29	99				God destroys Sodom and Gomorrah.
20:1	99				Abraham journeys toward the Negev and settles at Gerar (between Kadesh and Shur).

20:6	99				Abraham tells Abimelech that Sarah is his sister.
21:2	100	0			Isaac is born.
21:14	103	3			Abraham sends Hagar and Ishmael away.
21:22–34					Abraham enters into a covenant of peace with Abimelech and lives in Philistia.
22:9–12	118	18			God asks Abraham to offer Isaac as a sacrifice at Mt. Moriah.
23:1–2	137	37			Sarah dies at age 127.
24:1ff	140	40			Abraham sends a servant to find a wife for Isaac. Isaac marries Rebekah.
25:1–4					Abraham marries Keturah and has six more sons.
25:6					Abraham gives gifts to the sons of his concubines and sends them away from Isaac.
25:24–26	160	60	0		Jacob and Esau are born.
25:7ff	175	75	15		Abraham dies. Isaac and Ishmael bury him.
25:29–34		78	18		Esau sells his birthright to Jacob.
26:1–6					Isaac lives temporarily in Gerar due to famine at home.
26:7					Isaac tells Abimelech that Rebekah is his sister.
26:12–13					Isaac becomes rich by farming in Gerar.
26:12–23					Isaac has quarrels with Abimelech's men, so he moves to Shiba (which he names Beersheba, v. 33).
26:23–24					God appears to Isaac and reaffirms the covenant he had given to Abraham. Isaac makes peace with Abimelech.
26:34–35		100	40		Esau irritates Rebekah by taking two Hittite wives.
27:1–29					Jacob steals Esau's blessing.
27:41–28:29		137	77		Jacob flees Esau and begins working for Laban.
		144	84		Jacob marries Leah and Rachel.
29:31–30:21					Jacob has 10 sons.
30:22–24		151	91	0	Joseph is born (assuming Joseph was born at the end of the 14 years Jacob worked for Laban).
30:25–43					Jacob becomes rich working for Laban.
31:1–19					Jacob flees Laban.

				Event
32:24–32				Jacob wrestles with God and is renamed "Israel."
33:1–20				Jacob makes peace with Esau and settles in Shechem.
35:1				Jacob moves to Bethel.
35:16–20				Benjamin is born. Rachel dies.
37:2–36	168	108	17	Joseph dreams he will be a ruler but is sold into slavery.
35:29	180	120	29	Isaac dies.
41:46–47		121	30	Joseph becomes Pharaoh's minister over Egypt. First year of plenty.
41:53		127	36	Last year of plenty.
41:54		128	37	Famine starts.
46:1–7		130	39	Jacob goes to Egypt.
		135	43	Famine ends.
48:1–22		147	56	Jacob blesses Joseph's sons.
49:1–32		147	56	Jacob blesses his sons.
49:33		147	56	Jacob dies.
50:22–26			110	Joseph dies.

Measures in Genesis

Read about biblical weights and measures in Translation Notes below.

Length	
Cubit	From the elbow to the end of the fingers, about 18 inches.
Weight	
Shekel	About 0.37 troy ounces (11.5 grams), about the weight of two American nickels or two twenty-cent Euro coins. A shekel is also a silver coin of the same weight.
Sanctuary shekel	A slightly heavier shekel than the commercial one. As the extra amount is unknown, we use the same amount for conversion.
Capacity—Dry	Note: A dry measure quart or gallon is 16% larger than a liquid one.
Seah	About seven quarts. However, this seems a very large amount in light of Abraham telling Sarah to get "three seahs" of flour to bake bread for their three visitors (Gen. 18:6). So "seah" is commonly rendered in English Bible translations as "measure" (e.g., three measures).

Persons in Genesis
(in order of appearance)

Hebrew Name (English)	Key Facts	*Chapter*	Events in Genesis	*Chapter*
Adam (Man)	First Man	2	Committed first sin	3
Eve (To Live)	First Woman	2	Committed first sin	3
Cain & Abel	First brothers	4	Killed Abel	4
Seth (Appointed)	Replaced Abel Ancestor of Christ & Noah	5		
Enoch	Son of Seth	4	Walked with God, vanished	4
Noah (Console)	Ancestor of Christ 5 The only righteous man on earth when the ark was built	6	Built the ark and survived the flood 6–8 Received God's promise that he would never again destroy the earth through a flood 9 Got drunk, cursed Canaan 9	
Shem	Son of Noah 6 Ancestor of Abraham Ancestor of Christ 5, 10, 11		Populated the whole earth	9
Ham	Son of Noah 5 Father of Canaan 9		Populated the whole earth 9 Left his drunk father naked 9	
Japheth (God Will Enlarge)	Son of Noah	5	Populated the whole earth	9
Lot (Covering)	Abraham's nephew 11 Father of the Ammonites and Moabites 19		Chose to live in Sodom and had a troubled life there 13 Taken captive by the northern kings, rescued by Abraham 14 Rescued from Sodom by God's angels 19 Got drunk and had a son by each of his daughters 19	
Abram (Exalted Father) Abraham (Father of Many)	First patriarch of Israel Son of Terah 11 Husband of Sarah 11 Father of Ishmael and Isaac Ancestor of Christ 16, 21		See "Overlapping Lives of the Patriarchs" above	
Sarai Sarah (Princess)	Abraham's first wife 12 Ancestor of Christ 25		Gave Abraham Hagar to have a child 16 Drove out pregnant Hagar 16 Drove out Hagar & Ishmael 21	
Pharaoh (in Abraham's time)			Took Sarah as his wife Returned her when God struck his house with plagues 12	
Melchizedek	Priest of God Most High. King of Salem (Jerusalem) 14		Received tithe from Abraham 14	

Eliezer (God is Help)	Abraham's chief servant 15	Abraham's heir 16 Found a wife for Isaac 24
Hagar (Flight)	Sarah's maidservant Bore Ishmael 16	Bore Abraham's first son 16 Driven away by Sarah 21
Ishmael (God Hears)	Firstborn of Abraham (by Hagar) 16	Hated by Sarah and driven off with his mother 21
Abimelech*	King of Gerar in Abraham's time 20	Took Sarah to be his wife, but was warned by God to return her 20
Abimelech*	King of Gerar in Isaac's time 21	Protected Rebekah 26
Isaac (He Laughs)	Second patriarch of Israel 17 Firstborn of Abraham and Sarah 21 Ancestor of Christ 25	See "Overlapping Lives of the Patriarchs" above
Ephron	Hittite leader 23	Sold the cave of Machpelah to Abraham as a burial site 23
Rebekah	Sister of Laban 24 Wife of Isaac 24 Ancestor of Christ 25	Married Isaac after she was found by Abraham's servant in Paddan Aram 24 Gave birth to Esau & Jacob 25 Loved Jacob most and led him to deceive Isaac to get first son's blessing 27
Laban (White)	Grandson of Abraham's brother, Nahor 24 Rebekah's brother 27	Gave refuge to Jacob 29 Gave his daughters Leah and Rachel to Jacob in return for fourteen years of labor 29
Keturah (Perfumed One)	Abraham's wife after Sarah 25	Bore six sons of Abraham 25
Esau (Hairy), a.k.a. Edom (Red)	Firstborn son of Isaac 25 Father of the Edomites 36	Sold his birthright for a bowl of stew 25 Cheated out of his father's blessing by Jacob 27 Planned revenge, but Jacob fled 27, 28 Lived in peace with Jacob when he returned years later 32, 33
Jacob (He Grasps); a.k.a. Israel (He Struggles with God; or God Prevails)	Third patriarch of Israel Second son of Isaac 25 Ancestor of the 12 tribes of Israel 35 Ancestor of Christ 29	See "Overlapping Lives of the Patriarchs" above Cheated his older brother out of his blessing as firstborn. 27

* "Abimelech": A name taken by the king of the Philistines (as "Pharaoh" is taken by the king of Egypt).

Rachel	Laban's younger daughter 29	Bore Joseph & Benjamin 30, 35
Leah (Impatient?, Wild Cow?)	Laban's older daughter Jacob's first wife 29 Ancestor of Christ 29	Bore Jacob six sons and a daughter 29, 35
Reuben (See note, Gen. 29:32)	Jacob's first son (first by Leah) 29 Patriarch of the tribe of Reuben	Convinced his brothers not to kill Joseph but to put him in a cistern so he could rescue him later 37 Lost his status of firstborn because he slept with Bilhah, Jacob's concubine 49
Simeon (One Who Hears)	Jacob's second son (second by Leah) 29 Patriarch of the tribe of Simeon	With Levi, killed Hamor and his son and the men of Shechem in retaliation for the rape of Dinah and led the plunder of the city 34 Along with his brothers, sold Joseph into slavery 37 Kept in Egypt as a hostage until his brothers returned with Benjamin 44
Levi (Attached)	Jacob's third son (third by Leah) 29 Patriarch of the tribe of Levi, from whom the Levites descended	With Simeon, killed Hamor and his son and the men of Shechem in retaliation for the rape of Dinah and led the plunder of the city 34 Along with his brothers, sold Joseph into slavery 37
Judah (Praise)	Jacob's fourth son (fourth by Leah) 29 Patriarch of the tribe of Judah 29 Ancestor of Christ 29	Proposed the idea of selling Joseph into slavery 37 Had sons by Tamar, his oldest son's wife 38
Bilhah	Rachel's maidservant 30	Bore Dan & Napthali 30
Dan (He Has Vindicated)	Jacob's fifth son (first by Bilhah) 30 Patriarch of the tribe of Dan	Along with his brothers, sold Joseph into slavery 37
Napthali (My Struggle)	Jacob's sixth son (second by Bilhah) 30 Patriarch of the tribe of Napthali	Along with his brothers, sold Joseph into slavery 37
Zilpah	Leah's maidservant 30	Bore Gad & Asher 30
Gad (Good Fortune)	Jacob's seventh son (first by Zilpah) 30 Patriarch of the tribe of Gad	Along with his brothers, sold Joseph into slavery 37

Asher (Happy)	Jacob's eighth son (second by Zilpah) 30 Patriarch of the tribe of Asher	Along with his brothers, sold Joseph into slavery 37
Issachar (Reward)	Jacob's ninth son (fifth by Leah) 30 Patriarch of the tribe of Issachar	Along with his brothers, sold Joseph into slavery 37
Zebulun (Honor)	Jacob's tenth son (sixth by Leah) 30 Patriarch of the tribe of Zebulun	Along with his brothers, sold Joseph into slavery 37
Joseph (May He Add)	Jacob's eleventh son (first by Rebekah) 30 Patriarch of two tribes of Israel through his sons, Ephraim and Manasseh	Dreamed he would rule over his family 37 Sold into slavery by his brothers 37 Interpreted Pharaoh's dreams and ruled over Egypt 41–50 Forgave his brothers and brought Israel (a.k.a. Jacob) to Egypt 45–46
Benjamin (Son of My Right Hand)	Jacob's twelfth son (second by Rebekah) 35 Patriarch of the tribe of Benjamin	Used by Joseph to test his brothers 44
Hamor (He-ass)	Canaanite leader 33 Father of Shechem 33	Sold land to Jacob 33 Convinced his men to be circumcised 34 Killed by Simeon and Levi 34
Shechem (Shoulder, Slope)	Son of Hamor 34	Raped Dinah 34 Killed by Simeon and Levi 34
Potiphar	Pharaoh's captain of the guard 37	Purchased Joseph 37 Put him in prison 39
Hirah	Friend of Jacob An Adullamite 38	Served as Judah's messenger 38
[name unknown]	Judah's wife Daughter of Shua 38	Gave Judah three sons 38
Er (Watcher)	Judah's first son Tamar's husband 38	Acted wickedly and was killed by God 38
Onan (Strong)	Judah's second son 38	Would not sire a child by Tamar; killed by God 38
Shelah	Judah's third son 38	
Tamar (Palm Tree)	Er's wife 38 Ancestor of Christ 38	Had sons by Judah, her husband's father 38

Perez (Break Out)	Judah's fourth son, twin of Zerah (first by Tamar) 38 Ancestor of Christ 46	
Zerah (Scarlet, or Brightness)	Judah's fifth son, twin of Perez (second by Tamar) 38	
Asenath	Joseph's wife, daughter of Potiphera, a priest of On 41	Given by Pharaoh to Joseph for his wife 41
Manasseh (See Gen. 41:51 note)	Joseph's first son Patriarch of the tribe of Manasseh 41	Became the ancestor of a tribe of Israel, Manasseh, because he was adopted by Jacob 48
Ephraim (To Bear Fruit)	Joseph's second son Patriarch of the tribe of Ephraim 41	Became the ancestor of a tribe of Israel, Ephraim, because he was adopted by Jacob 48

Jewish Calendar

In addition to the Levitical feasts below, there were 12 new moon feasts, and every Sabbath was a day of complete rest.

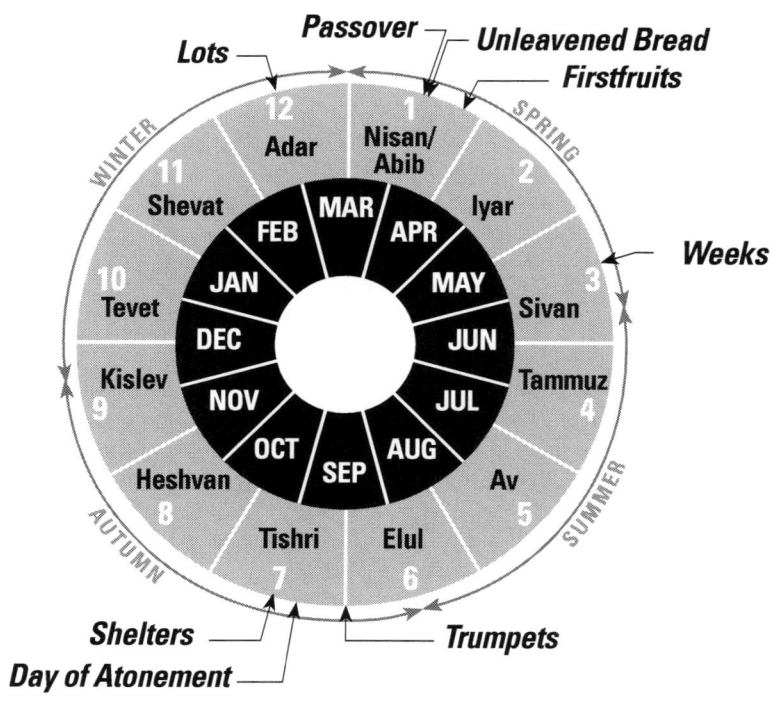

Subject Index

The subject begins at the cited verse.

Adultery	20:3
Ark, Noah's	6:13–8:19
Babel, Tower of	11:1–9
Blood, not eat	9:4
Cain and Abel	4:1–8
Children	
Blessing	4:25; 5:29; 30:1
Gift of God	4:1, 25; 17:16, 20; 29:32–35; 30:2, 6, 17–24; 33:5
Circumcision	17:10–14, 22–26; 21:4
Company, evil	19:15
Covenants	
Abrahamic	12:1–3; 13:14–17; 15:1–21; 17:1–27; 22:15–18
Reaffirmed to Isaac	26:3–6, 24
Reaffirmed to Jacob	35:12
Rainbow (a.k.a. Noahic)	9:8–17
Creation	1:1–25; 2:4–25
Death	3:19
Death Penalty	5:8; 9:5–6
Doubt, examples	12:12–13; 15:18; 18:12–14; 19:30; 20:2, 11; 26:6–7
Drunkenness	9:20–27; 19:30–38
Faith, examples of	6:22; 15:6; 16:13; 24:7; 48:21; 50:24
Family	2:23–24; 18:19
Forgiveness	33:4, 11; 44:5–15; 50:19–21
Garden of Eden	2:8–15; 3:22–24
Genealogies, descendants of	
Abraham	25:1
Adam and Eve	4:1
Adam	5:1
Edom	36:31
Esau	36:1
Jacob	35:22; 46:8
Nahor	22:20
Noah (Table of the Nations)	10:1
Seir	36:20
Shem	11:10

Holy Spirit	1:2
Husband	2:23-24
Intercession, example of	18:22-33
Jacob's Ladder	28:10-17
Justification	15:6
Man	
Creation	1:26-31; 2:7, 18-24; 5:1-2; 9:6
Dominion over the earth	2:15-17; 9:1-5
Fall (re: sin)	3:1-19
Maps	
Battle of the Kings	Chapter 14
The Life of Abraham	Chapter 12
The Life of Isaac	Chapter 26
The Life of Jacob	Chapter 27
The Life of Joseph	Chapter 37
Marriage	2:18-25; 3:16
Nephilim	6:4
Patriarchs, life spans of	5:3
Righteousness by faith	15:6
Sabbath	2:2-3
Satan	3:1-15
Sin	
Curse of	3:14-19
Desire of	4:6-7
Consequences, examples of	3:7-24; 4:9-14; 6:5-7
Sodom and Gomorrah, end of	19:1-29
Tithe	14:19
Work	3:17-19

Map Notes

We provide maps to give you a general idea of the movements of people. They are not perfectly accurate. However, you should be able to use them to help you find any location on a larger, more accurate map. Cities and towns not confirmed by modern archaeology are followed by a question mark. In these cases, when known, we present the location that either has the oldest tradition or is most commonly accepted today.

When maps show the location of people groups (e.g., Amorites, Ammonites), the location(s) shown are in the context of the year and place of the events. Some people groups had more than one location, and some moved. Thus, a group may appear in different locations on different maps.

Key to Genealogical Tables   07rl

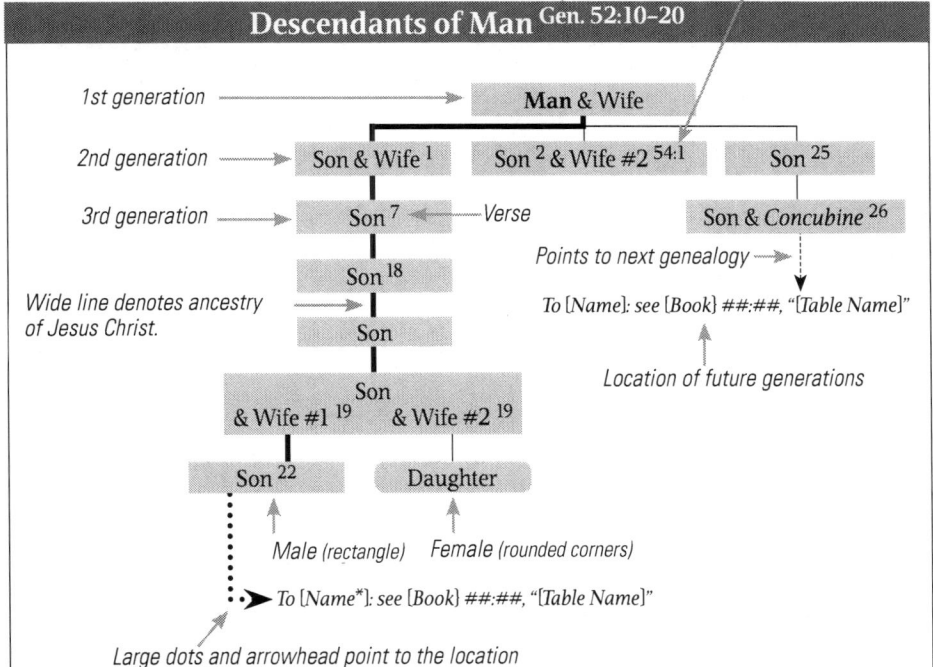

Verse References: If a box or line of text does not have a verse reference, the information comes from the last verse referenced to its left or above it.

Sexual Partners: Sexual partners are preceded by an ampersand ("&"). Wives are in roman typeface. Other sexual partners are in *italic* typeface.

Dual Relationship: a double arrow (◄—►) connecting two boxes with the same name indicates two relationships (e.g., daughter of one person, wife of another).

* Name of the last ancestor of Christ in the referenced table.

Our goal is to present you with a text that you can read as easily as you read any other twenty-first-century nonfiction work. Here are a few of the ways we do that. The Readable Bible is a literal translation[a] in the sense that each original language word is expressed in English. However, sometimes a literal translation is unlikely to communicate the writer's thought to a modern audience. For instance, people unfamiliar with ancient culture probably do not understand that the term "kiss the son" in Psalms 2:12 means to show him homage, to make a formal public acknowledgment of allegiance. So, when the literal translation might confuse or mislead today's reader, a thought-for-thought translation is presented and the literal translation is footnoted, or vice versa (unless the term is listed in the Nonliteral Words and Phrases Not Footnoted table).

As is common in modern translations, the words are not always expressed in the grammatical form of the original text when that creates awkward English. Instead, we present the grammatical form and sentence construction that we believe the writer would have chosen if he were a native English speaker. Occasionally, for clarity or ease of reading, we substitute a noun for a pronoun, or vice versa.

Many Hebrew words have several meanings. If an equally viable alternate term or phrase would give the text a significantly different sense or feel than the one given by the word we render, we provide the alternate in a notation.

Hebrew does not have comparative and superlative words. Rather, words are repeated to emphasize (give special force or prominence) or intensify (add force, degree or strength) a term. Rather than repeat words, we usually render the English term that expresses the comparative or superlative. The Hebrew repetition is footnoted.

Sometimes the author left out words that he knew his audience would have in their minds due to their familiarity with the context, culture, and language. Today, three thousand years later, English-speaking readers need these words added to the text. Thus, we supply them in *italics*. Occasionally, for clarity or ease of reading, we substitute a noun for a pronoun, or vice versa.

Italicized additions to the text are also meant to clarify the text or avoid confusion for readers who (1) are not familiar with Scripture truths and the history of Israel and (2) might not recognize when figures of speech (e.g., hyperbole, metaphors) are being used. For instance, Psalm 40:6 reads, "You did not desire sacrifice and offering." The Readable Bible inserts "only" before "sacrifice and offering" to make the reading reflect the true meaning of the statement.

Biblical weights and measures are presented in current equivalents. It is not uncommon for such estimates to differ by significant amounts, as ancient measures varied by time and place and archeological information is incomplete. We have used the most commonly accepted values. Coinage[b] can be expressed somewhat accurately in weight, but it is more difficult to translate its value into terms that relate accurately to today. The exact amount does not appear to be critical to the meaning of any passage.

---

a   The Old Testament is based primarily upon the Westminster Leningrad Codex, and the New Testament is based prmarily upon the 1904 Nestle tex,t with passages modified basd upon more recent manuscript evidence.

b   Coinage was simply pieces of metal used as a medium of exchange. The first government-issued coinage was made in about 600 BC, centuries after this book was written.

Format and Presentation Notes

Our goal is to present you with a text that you can read as easily as you read any other twenty-first-century nonfiction work. Here are a few of the ways we do that.

Chapter headings and other topical headings help keep you oriented and aid information searches. The contents table lists all these headings. Headings that are not part of sentences, and callout boxes that do not have verse numbers, are not part of the inspired text.

Some text has been moved to increase readability and clarity, to conform with modern paragraph construction practice, or to group like information in a single location. When text is moved to a different page, its original location is noted in its new location, and its new location is noted in its original location.

Verse numbers are grouped together when sentences and phrases have been rearranged to conform to English composition norms.

Personal pronouns that refer to God are not capitalized unless necessary for clarity (as there is no such distinction in the original manuscripts).

When a transliterated proper noun first appears in the text, its English translation is provided within parentheses like this: "Nod (i.e., Wandering)."

When the text has sentences describing genealogies (e.g., "X" gave birth to "Y."), the information is presented in a genealogical table.

Numerical data (e.g., age tables and object measurements) is presented in tables.

Items in series are sometimes presented in list format. These should be read down the first column and then down the next column.

Words and phrases that are not translated literally and appear more than twice are not footnoted. The literal translation is provided in the Nonliteral Words and Phrases Not Footnoted table.

In some instances it is not possible to make a certain translation because of our imperfect understanding of ancient language, and/or the apparent disorder of the text, and/or differences between ancient manuscripts. Such instances are annotated (e.g., "the Hebrew is not clear"), sometimes with an alternative translation.

The slash between words in a footnotes represents "or," or" and/or."

Ancient writings use "said" to indicate a direct quotation. Today we use quotation marks for the same purpose. Thus, when the Hebrew reads, "The Lord spoke to Moses, saying [quote]," The Readable Bible reads, "The Lord said to Moses, "[quote]."

Greek and Hebrew word transliterations are of the root word or the word in the text. They are meant to give insight into the meaning of the text, and help the reader get started if they would like to research the word.

Dates are added in italics. Despite the anachronistic problem of using "BC" and "AD" in biblical documents, it aids understanding sufficiently to warrant its use. Bible dates are generally considered accurate plus or minus two or three years.

Tables, charts, and bulletted lists occasionally appear in the midst of a direct quote. The information contained in them includes all the thought of that part of the direct quote and replaces it.   08rl

Nonliteral Words and Phrases Not Footnoted

The word "said" in Hebrew is oftentimes rendered as an equivalent word that introduces the feeling and/or emotion with which the words were spoken (e.g., announced, asked, answered, called to/out, cautioned, claimed, complained, confirmed, continued, declared, directed).

We follow the common English Bible translation practice of inserting words that are not in the Hebrew text at the start of a sentence to facilitate smooth reading (e.g., "so," "now," "then," "when," "rather"). Thus, "then" does not mean the following event directly followed the preceding event, though it might have. The reader must use their own judgment.

When a place name occurs without part of its normal English title we add the title (e.g., e, "Jordan" becomes "Jordan River," "Negev" becomes "Negev Desert."

We do not footnote the literal translation in the following instances.

Readable Bible Translation	Literal Translation
All living creatures	All flesh
Be angry	Let your anger burn
Before	In the sight of
[Country name] (e.g., Egypt)	Land of [country name] (e.g., Land of Egypt)
Descendants	Descendants after you; descendants with you generations throughout their generations
Died	Gathered to his people
Everybody	All the persons
Family history/record	Generations, generations of the sons
Forever	Throughout your generations, generation to generation
Intimate relations	Knew. The verb implies intimate knowledge, sexual relations.
Israelites	Children/people/sons of Israel
Looked up	Lifted his eyes
Made love to	Knew (Hebrew: *yada*)
[Name] lived (e.g., Jacob lived)	The days of [name] were (e.g., the days of Jacob were)
Named [pronoun] [name] (e.g., Named him Jacob)	Called his/its name [name] (e.g., called his name Jacob)
Person/them/they	He/him replaced when the text is gender neutral.
Pregnant	With child
Saw	Lifted their eyes and saw
See him myself	Set my eyes on
Slept with	lay down (Hebrew: *shakab*), go in (Hebrew: *bo*)

The [group of people] (e.g., the Hittites)	Sons of [first father of the group] (e.g., the sons of Heth)
These are the [position] (e.g., these are the chiefs)	These are the names of the [position] (e.g., these are the names of the chiefs)
Well	Well of water
Wild animals	Beasts of the field

Made in the USA
Lexington, KY
26 September 2017